100 WORSHIP ACTIVITIES FOR CHILDREN

100 Worship Activities for Children

CHRIS LEACH

EASTBOURNE

First published 2000
Reprinted 2002

ISBN   0 85476 908 0

Illustrations by Paul Leach.

Published by
KINGSWAY COMMUNICATIONS LTD
Lottbridge Drove, Eastbourne, BN23 6NT, England.
Email: books@kingsway.co.uk

Book design and production for the publishers by
Bookprint Creative Services, P.O. Box 827, BN21 3YJ, England.
Printed in Great Britain.

Contents

Acknowledgements   10
Introduction   11

Advent
  1. Follow That Star!   23
  2. Joyful Procession   25
  3. Worship A Cappella   26
  4. Candle Countdown   28
  5. The Jesse Tree   30

Christmas
  6. He Walked Where I Walk   35
  7. Give Him Your Heart   37
  8. Party Time!   39
  9. Paper Chains   40
10. With Love From ...   41
11. Some Hay in a Manger   42

New Year
12. A Prayer Tree   47
13. Hasn't She Grown!   48
14. Hopes and Fears   50
15. Instant Psalm   53

Epiphany
16. Gold, Frankincense and Myrrh   57
17. Shine, Jesus, Shine   59
18. Starry Sky   61
19. An Object Lesson   63

The Baptism of Christ
20. Say That Again   67
21. Follow Me!   69
22. Teddy Bears' Picnic   71

Candlemas
23. Character Trays   75
24. Face Forward   77
25. Best Foot Forward   79

Lent
26. Dust and Ashes   83
27. Time to be Holy   85
28. All Stations   87
29. Back to the Fold   89
30. Slavery to Freedom   91
31. The Bridge to Life   93
32. Flower Disarranging!   96
33. The Prodigal Son   98
34. Dirty Hands   100

Mothering Sunday
35. Heartfelt Thanks   105
36. Come for Coffee   107
37. Cocktails   109
38. Hidden Kindness   110

Palm Sunday
39. Palm Crosses   115
40. Going Up to Worship   117

41. The Way of the Cross 120
42. Feet First 122

Good Friday
43. Demolition 127
44. Hot Cross Buns 129
45. Caught Red-Handed 130
46. Two Become One 131
47. Seeds of Hope 1 133

Easter
48. Make Some Noise! 137
49. A Little More Noise 139
50. Scrunchie Praise 140
51. The Easter Candle 141
52. What Comes Out ... 142
53. Seeds of Hope 2 144
54. Action Creed 145

Ascension
55. The Royal Family 149
56. Worship His Majesty 151
57. Jigsaw Praise 153
58. Egging Us On 155
59. Reflected Glory 157
60. Crowned with Glory Now 158

Pentecost
61. Dressing Up 163
62. Happy Birthday, Dear Church 164
63. Feeling the Draught 165
64. Pass the Parcel 167
65. Speaking in Tongues 168
66. The Spirit at Work 169
67. Light the Fire Again 170
68. Flowers in the Desert 172

Trinity Sunday
69. Trinity Leaves   177
70. The Writing's on the Wall   178
71. Graffiti Intercessions   180
72. God Is ...   182

New School Year
73. School Photos   187
74. A Hands-on Approach   189
75. Jesus Goes to School   190

Harvest
76. Sight and Sound   195
77. Dolphin Music   197
78. Harvest Hip-Hop   198
79. What a Load of Rubbish!   200
80. A Smashing Time   202
81. Do It Yourself   203
82. Out of the Mouths of Babes   204
83. Falling Leaves   205
84. The 'Wow!' Factor   207
85. Patchwork Praise   208

Gift Day
86. Envelopes   213
87. Envelopes, but not Stationary!   215
88. Kids' Packs   216

All Saints
89. Passing the Baton   221
90. On Yer Bike!   223
91. For All the Saints   225
92. Local Heroes   227

Christ the King
93. King of Kings   231

94. Reign in Me 232
95. Kings and Queens 234
96. King? What King? 235
97. Stained-Glass Windows 237

Missions
98. Coming ... 241
99. ... and Going 243
100. So I Send You 245

Subject Index 247
Song Index 249

Acknowledgements

I would like to express my heartfelt thanks to my husband John for his confidence in me, for his support, practical wisdom and encouragement to keep going and to serve up to others what is my bread and butter. Without him this book would still be a pipe-dream.

I also want to honour the many other friends and fellow workers who have suggested ideas or background information for inclusion in this book, whether or not their ideas actually made it into print. So a big 'thank you' to Dhoe and Peter Craig-Wild, John Gunstone, Cate Hall, Karen Hamblin, Sue Kennedy, Debbie Le Sueur, Liz Lunn, David Mann, Angela Thompson, and Hazel Wilson.

And thanks, too, to the children and young people of St James' Styvechale, in Coventry, among whom most of these ideas were first tried out.

To God be the glory, now and for ever.

Introduction

Why seasons?

Many years ago my husband had a friend who was the lift operator in the hospital where he worked. He was a simple soul (the lift operator, that is), and used to take great delight in responding, when asked how he was, by saying, 'Well, you know. Up and down!'

The fact is that life *is* up and down. We all go through a mixture of special times and ordinary times, with some bad times thrown in too. The seasons of the year which we see in nature around us go through cycles, with the colours changing from bright green to golden yellow to black and white to pink. Our own lives are full of ups and downs, through birthdays, funerals, anniversaries, holidays and the ordinary days of just getting on with it. Life's like that.

The church has long recognised in its worship that life is like that. From the time when the earliest Christians set aside Sunday, the day after the Jewish Sabbath, as a special day to remember the resurrection of Jesus, times and seasons have been important to Christians. Even the Jewish faith, from which Christianity was born, was lived in cycles of feasts and festivals, sabbaths and pilgrimages. Few Christians today would forget to celebrate Christmas or Easter, but there is so much more to it than that. And surely the tendency in some circles to forget the whole thing, with rhetoric like 'every day is Easter Day', is just plain silly. Every day isn't our birthday, but one day is, and so we celebrate it (or bemoan it!) and get on with real life for the rest of the year.

The 'church calendar' dates from the earliest history of the church. Many of the ancient Jewish festivals were taken over by the first Christians and turned into celebrations of events in the life of Jesus. In the fourth century, when persecution of the church ended, Christians were free to worship much more publicly, and, particularly in the city of Jerusalem, great festivals, processions and rituals became popular, often using the actual sites from Jesus' life. The church year gradually took shape, and it has evolved slowly into the one used in many churches today.

Not only does following the calendar give us a run-through of the life and ministry of Jesus, it also allows us to experience different things at different times: celebration at Easter and Christmas, but sorrow for our sins during Lent, hope and expectation during Advent, and so on. And of course it contains some long periods of time where we're not particularly encouraged to 'feel' much at all, but simply to get on with the task of worshipping God and living for him.

This book is designed to be used with children not only in churches that already follow the church calendar, but also in churches that might want to explore more of the riches it gives us. I have based the sections on the calendar of the *Revised Common Lectionary* used by most Anglican churches nowadays, but I have taken the liberty of missing out a few dates (mostly because they fall on a weekday, and so you are unlikely to have any children's ministry on those days), and also adding a few important dates from the 'secular' calendar, such as New Year, new school term, and so on. Some important days do often fall during the week, but I have included these because many churches would simply celebrate them on the closest Sunday. Where an event has a set date I have included it, but many of them revolve around Easter, and so vary from year to year.

It has become customary in some churches to use different colours to mark the different events or seasons. Some clergy and lay ministers would wear robes of the appropriate colour, and fabrics and decorations in the church would be changed to match. Even without going that far, flowers or other decorations could reflect the seasonal colours.

Purple is a colour associated with mourning or penitence, and would be used for Advent and Lent, and often for funeral services too. White or gold is used for special celebrations, such as the major festivals of Christmas and Easter, and the seasons around them. Red, the colour of fire, is used for Pentecost, but it also represents blood, and so is used during Holy Week, and for the feast days of saints who were martyred for their faith. Green is the 'ordinary' colour, and is used when nothing else special is happening, to represent our slow and steady growth in our discipleship.

These are the basic colours, but the really exacting can take it all much further: pink or rose for the visit of the Angel to Mary on the fourth Sunday in Advent, blue for healing services, colourless sackcloth during Lent, and so on. Colour can be useful, but we may not want to get too fussy about it!

Why different colours? Simply because they can change atmospheres, as anyone with any background in lighting for the stage can tell you. The world around us changes colour as the seasons move through their course, so why not the church as well? The whole purpose of the church calendar, as I've said, is to get us away from the boring and untrue idea that every week is the same, and colour can be a powerful way of emphasising the different seasons and their distinctions.

Each seasonal section is introduced by a brief paragraph on what it is about, and what some of the emphases might be in celebrating it. Then I give a few practical ideas for worship with children, either in an all-age setting in church, or in their own groups. Use the ideas if they work for you, but use them creatively, and don't feel you have to stick too rigorously to the calendar. My main aim is to help our children rediscover the often-neglected riches of the times and seasons of the year, and so to be enriched themselves in their Christian discipleship.

How to use this book

You will see the ideas have been arranged under twenty different sections, relating to the event or season in the calendar. Many of the ideas will only be useful when you are celebrating the particular season under which they have been placed, but others could work at different times if you were to put a slightly different spin on them. And a few would be useful throughout the year: for instance, penitence, or saying sorry to God for our sin, is a particular focus during the season of Lent, but should be a part of what we do whenever we come together to worship. Feel free to use some of those suggestions all through the year.

Each idea gives you some information before you start, beginning with the *aim* for the session. What is this idea about, and what are we trying to achieve by using it? Then a *setting* is suggested. Most commonly this is either your children's ministry groups or an all-age service (or both), although some of the ideas have been used as school assemblies or even at home in the family. Some are obviously more appropriate for younger or older children, and a few of the ideas require more than one week: all this is clearly indicated.

Next the *equipment* you'll need is suggested, and I have tried to think of everything so you have no surprises when you actually try the idea out. However, it is worth thinking carefully through what you're going to need, particularly if you want to adapt my ideas in any way, which you are welcome to do. Finally I have indicated any specific or unusual Bible passages upon which the idea is based, although I haven't been too conscientious about this, assuming that most children's workers do know where to find, for example, the resurrection!

Then comes the idea itself, but with scope for flexibility too. A few ideas might provide material for a whole service or children's group session, but most are meant to be just one activity within a service of worship. The ideas are simply ideas: there is no copyright on them, and you are encouraged not to use them slavishly but adapt them according to your needs, the number of children, their spiritual awareness, and so on. But however you do use them, remember it is important that people meet God through them. I don't believe our children's ministries need *just* good ideas: rather we need to lead children to a profound encounter with the living God.

Many of these ideas are not new, but seek to help children (and adults) rediscover some of the richness of ancient tradition. The history of the church contains a series of pendulum swings from one extreme to another: rich and vibrant liturgy came to be seen by some as empty superstition, and so austerity and a focus on the Scriptures came to the fore, until another group of Christians sought to reintroduce some colour and spectacle into what they saw as dull and cerebral, and so the swings continued. Many present day Evangelicals have been brought up with a Reformed fear of symbols, images and icons, and have focused on the truth of the written word. But we are seeing in our times another pendulum swing as more and more Christians have rediscovered for themselves the real value of much of this forbidden fruit, and have discovered as well the fact that to reach men and women in our postmodern world we have to use all the riches of the church's heritage. Take candles, for example. Many churches, in an attempt not to be 'churchy' and thereby to appeal to postmodern people, have banned them from church services, failing to note that many shops in the High Street are now selling candles in their hundreds!

So this book, as well as suggesting ideas which I or my friends have thought up and used ourselves, is also full of church tradition. I have tried to be like the teacher 'who brings out of his storeroom new treasures as well as old'

(Matthew 13:52), and I have tried to keep Jesus central to everything I suggest, using the ideas to point to him and not to themselves.

I do, of course, suggest fairly frequently during the book that children might sing, and it will remain a valuable way for them to express their worship. But please don't make the mistake of thinking it is the only way: God has given us so much more with which to worship him than songs. Some people reading this book will feel it demands far too much of the children, and is not related to their experience. Many of these ideas do presuppose that children will be able to pray out loud in public from an early age, hear God speaking to them, know how to pray for and minister to one another and even to adults, use gifts of the Spirit such as tongues, and so on. I am aware of two things: first I know from my travels that this is not the level of discipleship at which many children's groups are functioning, but second I know from my own ministry and that of others committed to fully charismatic children's work that nothing in this book is impossible. I know this to be true because most of these ideas have been used in real settings: I didn't just dream them up to make up the hundred!

I don't want to de-skill you, but I do want to challenge you to take your children further, because I am convinced that where children are slow to move in the gifts of the Spirit it is always because of hesitancy on the part of the adults who lead them, or, more accurately, who don't lead them, rather than any inherent limitations in children's spirituality.

Jesus told us that to enter the kingdom of heaven adults need to become like little children: working with them has convinced me again and again of the truth of those words. My book *Children's Ministry and the Holy Spirit*[1] provides a step-by-step account of how to get children moving in the gifts and power of the Holy Spirit, and I am sure that what is expected

---

[1] Chris Leach, *Children's Ministry and the Holy Spirit* (Kingsway Publications, 2001).

of children in the ideas I've suggested here is merely normal Christianity, not some advanced class for superstars.

What about the leaders? Clearly you are leaders, and hopefully you will have more experience and maturity than the children. At times you will need to lead the sessions, but for the health of the group you will at other times need to participate with the children as equals. Expect God to touch you through these ideas, ask the children to pray for you, and get stuck in, rather than observing from the sidelines. Nothing is better designed to limit children's spirituality than leaders who remain aloof and unconnected.

But is it worship?

'When I use a word,' said Humpty Dumpty to Alice, 'it means just what I choose it to mean!' Nowhere is this more true than when trying to define 'worship' in the contemporary church. One of my pet hates is the 'worship leader' who, perhaps half-an-hour into a service, after the congregation has sung a hymn or two, listened to scriptures being read, and joined in prayer together, announces that now they are going to have 'a time of worship'. What on earth does he think they have been doing for the last half hour? But almost equally annoying are pious assertions that of course 'all of life is worship', a statement which, while theologically and ideally true, is pretty meaningless. If everything a Christian does is worship, or at least should be, what do we call those moments of intimacy with God, often during singing, which are extra special, and which can often leave us significantly different as Christians afterwards? Clearly I shall need to explain what I mean by the word 'worship' in this book, lest some of my readers think they've been cheated, and this or that idea isn't worship at all. The worship leader described above is using a very narrow definition: worship equals singing songs. But the other view, that for the Christian the whole of life is worship, has defined the word in such a wide way that it is almost completely robbed of meaning. I've tried to steer a middle course.

The word 'worship' has somewhere at its root the 'worth' we give to God as we focus on him, tell him how much we love him, and offer our lives to him. As we draw closer to him we are enabled to bring more of ourselves into the act of worship: our emotions and wills are stirred, and we may use our bodies and our senses as well as our voices. The closer we get to God, the more aware we will become of the beat of his heart and his concerns for us and our world, and of course the more time we spend in his presence focused on him, the more we will grow to be like him. Worship has an outward-looking dimension as well as drawing inwardly closer to God.

Clearly one of the contexts in which worship can take place is a church service, but not everything that happens in that service will lead us into the intimate presence of God, although hopefully much of it will. I have sought to reflect a wide understanding of worship, where children can be involved in body, mind and spirit, but where they don't necessarily reach the point of rapt wonder, love and praise every time.

My church heritage is Anglican, and it is from this background that I understand worship to be anything we do which helps us orientate ourselves towards God, recognising the value of liturgy, prayers, sacraments, pictures, sound, light and colour, fabrics and clothing and above all action to connect us with him. Some church traditions have, for the most understandable of reasons, rejected all or some of these worship ingredients: my aim in this book is to reintroduce readers (and even Anglican readers who have not fully appreciated the riches of their own tradition) to a much fuller and more holistic understanding of what worship is. 'Worship' isn't some period or even a magic moment within a service: it should pervade the whole of the service, and, yes, all of our lives. There may be special moments in worship when we really do engage with God at a deep level, but it is not true to say that without such moments we are not worshipping.

Thus some of what this book suggests is quite ordinary. To wave a palm cross about as we sing, for example, will probably not lead to an instant state of rapture. But it will, especially if it is a new thing to do, enrich the worship of a child, perhaps give her or him a new insight, or touch an emotion which the mere words of the song cannot. More and more I have come to realise it is what we *do* in worship that touches us far more deeply than what we say, sing or hear, and so this book suggests some ways in which a child's whole being can become involved and turned towards God.

One final point about this book: I hope and pray that it will be a means through which the life-giving power of the Holy Spirit can touch children and adults alike. Many of the ideas are not new; they have a long and honoured tradition in some parts of the church. But rarely were they ever used to help children encounter God, only to help them learn about him. My husband was once involved in planning a Pentecost service for children where someone had the idea of cutting out lots of shiny flame shapes from red, yellow and orange foil, and dropping them on children's heads 'to represent the Holy Spirit coming on them'. John's suggestion was that they dispense with the coloured flames and just invite the Spirit to come! My desire in the book is, in effect, that we use the foil *and* welcome the Holy Spirit. There is much on the market which can teach children about wind, fire, and so on, using kites, electric fans and the like. I have no desire to use symbols *instead of* the reality, but as means through which the reality might be experienced.

Lead the activities with sensitivity and openness to the Holy Spirit, and not just as activities for their own sake; lead them as though they are worship, and you'll find they can become worship. If you work with that aim in mind, I'm sure you will find, as we did, that God is pleased to use them in growing his young (and not so young) disciples.

So have a go, try things out, refuse to limit the children or the Holy Spirit, and enjoy the book!

Advent

No. 2 'Joyful Procession'

The season of Advent dates from fifth-century Gaul, where the six Sundays before Christmas were kept as a special season of preparation, although this was later reduced to the four-Sunday pattern we now have. The first Sunday (known as 'Advent Sunday') falls at the very end of November or the beginning of December. The season has a dual focus: the preparation for and anticipation of the celebration of the coming of Christ at Christmas, and a chance to look forward to the final return of Jesus. Like Lent, it usually has a penitential element, and it encourages us to be prepared and ready to meet with our Saviour when he comes.

Advent is one of the richest seasons of the Christian year, and it has abounded with imagery and themes throughout the

21

history of the church. The 'Advent Antiphons' would have been used on the final seven days before Christmas Eve, and consisted of prayers using different titles for God from the Old Testament, and which have now been written up as the hymn 'O Come O come Emmanuel'. Advent sermons in the past would have centred on the 'Four Last Things': death, judgement, hell and heaven. However, you might prefer just to think about Christmas! More recently the second Sunday of Advent has been used as Bible Sunday, a time to focus on God's gift of the Scriptures to us.

In the latest church calendar there is the additional innovation of having four Sundays *before* Advent, the fourth of which is the feast of Christ the King, so it is possible, in line with all the High Street shops, to begin looking to Christmas earlier! Red may be used as the colour for these four Sundays, while Advent itself is purple.

1. Follow That Star!

Aim

To build up a sense of anticipation and expectancy in worship.

Setting

Ideally in church, although this could also work in the room where children's groups meet.

Equipment

Large star made of silver or gold foil; Blu-tak.

Outline

On Advent Sunday talk about our waiting for Christmas and the gradual build-up of excitement. Stick the star somewhere prominent but at the back of the church/room, and talk about how we're going to follow it to the stable.

Each week put the star up in a different place, getting gradually closer to the front. Build up a sense of excitement by mapping the star's progress, and talking about how much further it has to travel. It can finally have pride of place at the front of the church, or over the crib if you have one, on Christmas morning. We used this at home as a family, moving the star daily rather than weekly, and feeling our excitement build each day.

Strictly speaking the star should arrive in time for

Epiphany, not Christmas. Instead of a star, one church we know used three life-size cardboard kings, suitably decorated, who gradually made their way to the front during Advent. Kings, of course, should definitely wait until Epiphany.

2. Joyful Procession

Aim

To engender a sense of journey and pilgrimage.

Setting

All-age services, or possibly children's groups.

Outline

Quite simply, while singing a song or hymn, walk around the church. The tradition of singing in procession goes back at least to the Psalms, when people would process joyfully into Jerusalem to worship. The 'Songs of Ascents' (Psalms 120–134) would almost certainly have been used in this way. To sing on the move occasionally, rather than remaining static in seats or pews, somehow feels different, and can really capture the imagination of children.

Some purpose to the procession is helpful, for example processing to the font for a baptism, or even out at the end for coffee. Songs or hymns which speak of pilgrimage or journey are helpful: 'We are marching (Siya Hamba)' is a good example.

Many churches use processions on all manner of special occasions, but Advent does seem to be a particularly good time, with its sense of making our way towards Christmas and the final return of Jesus.

3. Worship A Cappella

Aim

To show that the worship we offer now is nothing compared to the worship we'll one day offer Jesus face to face.

Setting

All-age services.

Equipment

This will only work if you have a fairly substantial worship team: to use a single church organist will make the point for adults, but may not be too child-friendly!

Outline

Begin by apologising for the fact that your musicians haven't yet turned up (some service leaders may be well-practised in this!) and say you're going to wait. After a brief wait, and before things get too out of hand, decide to start anyway. Get a single guitarist or vocalist planted in the congregation to lead, badly, a time of sung worship, and make as brave an attempt at it as you can.

Suddenly and dramatically your regular musicians appear from the back, pick up their instruments, and join in with as much gusto as possible.

After the song slot has ended, make the point that our

worship now is in a time of waiting: we do the best we can, but when King Jesus appears we'll *really* worship.

4. Candle Countdown

Aim

To build up excitement and anticipation towards Christmas.

Setting

In church, or possibly in children's group rooms. This is also something which many families do at home.

Equipment

Equipment for making an Advent wreath; wax tapers.

Outline

Advent is a time of anticipation and growing excitement, and this can be heightened, especially for children, by anything which 'counts down' to Christmas. Advent wreaths have been used in this way, not least on *Blue Peter*, for many years. Whatever the design, it consists of four candles arranged around a larger central one. Traditionally the four outer candles are purple, the liturgical colour for Advent, with the central one white, although red is often used instead of purple. The whole thing is often decorated with flowers, or with Christmas holly and ivy, and should be given pride of place at the front of your gathering for worship.

On the first Sunday of Advent, at the start of the service or session, one of the candles is lit; on the second, two; on the third, three, and so on. The final central candle is lit during the Christmas morning service. Children can be chosen to light the candles (try to avoid doing it by birthdays – you'll get the same children every year!) and a moment of prayer can follow the lighting.

5. The Jesse Tree

Aim

To discover more about the Old Testament background to Jesus, and to build up anticipation towards Christmas.

Setting

In church, or in the children's group room.

Equipment

A large leafless tree branch, set in a pot to look like a growing tree; card; play dough; felt pens; cotton.

Outline

The Jesse Tree is an ancient tradition which can be used to heighten children's understanding and anticipation of Christmas. You can begin this exercise on Advent Sunday, or alternatively you could begin earlier, since the new church calendar has four Sundays before Advent, as well as the four of Advent itself.

Select either four or eight Old Testament stories, and tell one each week in the children's groups, making sure that you make the link with Jesus and his coming at Christmas. Stories you could choose might be the Creation, Noah and the ark, Joseph saving his family from the famine, Moses putting up the snake in the desert for people to be healed, David rescuing his people by killing the giant Goliath, Esther speaking to the king on behalf of her people, Jonah being sent with a message which would save the people of Nineveh from God's anger, and John the Baptist telling the people to get ready for Jesus. The children can then make little symbols to hang on the tree for each week, beginning with the lower branches and working up towards the top centre. So, for example, during a week on creation they could make sun, moon and stars, either by colouring pictures or modelling play dough, or even bringing in little models of animals and birds. For Noah you could make little boats and rainbows, for Joseph some sheaves of corn or stars, for Moses some snakes covered in bronze-coloured metallic foil, etc. You could talk about God's good world being spoilt and waiting for rescue, God saving those who believe, and his promise never again to flood the world, and so on, linking the stories to Jesus our Saviour.

Depending on where it is, you could hang the pictures or models on the tree at the end of the service, and use prayers around the theme of the week. It might not be a bad idea for the adults to study the same subjects in their teaching, so that the whole church is on the same journey towards the birth of Jesus.

On Christmas Day, something representing Jesus could be put at the very top of the tree. It could be used in a different way for New Year (see Outline No. 12).

Christmas

No. 7 'Give Him Your Heart'

You probably don't need me to explain to you what Christmas is all about! Christians wanted an occasion to celebrate the birth of Jesus, and lacking much information about exactly when to celebrate it, they landed on the pagan winter solstice festival of *Natalis Solis Invicti* (the Birth of the Invincible Sun) which had been founded in Rome by the emperor Aurelius in AD 274. After all, if everyone else was having a party, why couldn't we, to celebrate the birth of the Son of Righteousness?

Luke's Gospel is our greatest source of information about Jesus' birth, with the accounts of the annunciation, the census and the birth of Jesus in Bethlehem, and the visit of the shepherds. The church down the years has elaborated the story by bringing on Matthew's three kings at the same time as the shepherds, which makes a lovely tableau for a nativity scene, but is probably historically inaccurate. The kings may not have arrived for another couple of years, and anyway liturgically they are not featured until the feast of Epiphany.

Christmas revolves around the giving and receiving of gifts: God's gift to us in Jesus, and ours to each other in friendship. The mood is one of celebration and joy, and the liturgical colour used is that of major celebrations: gold or white. It is good practice, although it flies in the face of our consumerist culture, not to anticipate Christmas too much, so that the day itself feels like the end of the season rather than its beginning. But with the shops beginning their run up from about October, we're probably fighting a losing battle!

6. He Walked Where I Walk

Aim

To praise and intercede in the light of Jesus' total identification with us as human beings.

Setting

An all-age service.

Equipment

Several pairs of boys' and men's shoes, representing different age groups: for example, a pair of baby's bootees, toddler's first shoes, school shoes, trainers, and adult shoes. Using pen or clip art, put three footprints on an A4 sheet of paper, one of which should have the words 'He walked where I walk' inside the footprint. Photocopy the A4 sheets, one per person, and cut them into individual footprints. The blank footprints should be given out, two per person, along with a pen, as people arrive. Don't give out the footprints with the words on.

Outline

Christmas is the natural time to focus on the 'incarnation' of Jesus, in other words his taking up humanity and entering our world in order to experience all that we live through. Talk about this, and the fact that there's nothing that happens to us, good or bad, in which Jesus doesn't share. Obviously you

can't get too specific on this. Jesus presumably never experienced the frustration of not being able to find a parking space,
or having his computer crash, and he never grew to be elderly,
but the point is that our God is not a distant figure, but one
who has lived as a human, as the Book of Hebrews stresses.

At some point early in the service (even perhaps as people
are arriving) invite everyone to write or draw on their two
footprints what they think are the best and worst aspects of
being the age they are. Parents will need to do this with young
children, and for babies. They should keep their footprints for
later.

Later on in the service, line up all the pairs of shoes at the
front, making the point that Jesus grew up through all these
different stages of life. An even more dramatic way of making
the same point in an all-age service would be to invite forward and line up behind the shoes in age order all the males in
the congregation aged between 0 and 33, and invite people to
visualise Jesus at each of these ages.

Invite everyone to walk to the front, find a pair of shoes
most closely representing their own age, and put their paper
feet into them, the good thing in one and the bad in the other,
remembering as they do so that Jesus has been where they are,
and has enjoyed the good things and been hurt over the bad.
After a song, such as 'Christmas, it's Christmas', 'You laid
aside your majesty', 'For the joys and for the sorrows', or 'He
walked where I walk', move into a time of prayer where you
can give thanks to Jesus for his human identification with us,
and pray for any people or groups of people who might particularly need Jesus alongside them as they walk through
difficult times.

As people leave the service, give each person one of the
third paper feet, with 'He walked where I walk' written on, as
a take-home reminder of the theme.

7. Give Him Your Heart

Aim

To emphasise Jesus as the heart of Christmas.

Setting

Children's groups or all-age services.

Equipment

Enough hearts for everyone, about 5 cm square, cut out from red card; a crib or manger with some straw and a baby doll in, possibly the one in your church crib scene if you have one; enough red heart-shaped balloons for each family (we got ours from Balloon Ideas, Hinckley Farm, Radbourne, Kirk Langley, Derby DE6 4LY, 01332 824268, www.balloonideas.co.uk).

Outline

Use the experience of receiving Christmas gifts to talk about how much the Father has given for us in sending Jesus into our world. In many churches there will typically be a whole variety of people present who wouldn't normally be there. The little red cardboard hearts can be used to challenge people to respond by offering gifts back to God. The heart might symbolise for them a first commitment to Jesus, a return to faith, or some specific area of surrender. At an appropriate point in the service, people can be invited forward simply to place the hearts in the crib as a sign of their love or surrender.

At the end of the service give each family or individual a heart-shaped balloon to take away to remind them throughout the rest of the Christmas period of God's gift to them and theirs to him.

8. Party Time!

Aim

To turn your church service into a party to celebrate Jesus' birthday.

Setting

Children's groups or all-age services.

Equipment

Balloons; party-poppers; cake, etc.

Outline

In the middle of an otherwise ordinary song-slot, lead unexpectedly into 'Happy birthday to you, happy birthday dear Jesus' and erupt into clapping, cheering, party-poppers, letting down balloons from a net in the ceiling, and any other party activities that seem appropriate. Continue with loud party music, and share in cake, or jelly and ice-cream. This might lead into more celebratory music, such as 'Christmas, it's Christmas' and 'Heaven invites you to a party'.

9. Paper Chains

Aim

To celebrate and give thanks for the good things we have received.

Setting

All-age services.

Equipment

One piece of coloured gummed paper (the sort used to make paper chains) for everyone present; pens; Blu-tak.

Outline

Talk about the things we have to say thank you to God for today. Invite everyone to write a thank you prayer on their piece of paper, and remind the older ones to help the little ones by writing their suggestions for them.

When everyone has done this, get the whole congregation to say their thank you aloud on the count of three. Encourage them to be enthusiastic in their thanks. Begin to join up the separate pieces of paper into long chains, and use the finished chains to add to the decorations you already have around the church. Lead into some lively carols or songs which express thanks to God for Jesus.

10. With Love From...

Aim

To help people express their thanksgiving to God.

Setting

All-age services.

Equipment

Gift tags, either bought or made from old Christmas cards with pinking shears and ribbon; felt pens.

Outline

This is an alternative way to offer praise from Outline No. 9. During a time of prayer, invite people to write thank you prayers, or words of adoration and worship to Jesus, on their gift tags. Young children will again need help from older people. These can then be brought forward and hung on a Christmas tree as a physical act of worship.

You could pick ten at random and read them out as prayers, and do the same with another ten at each Christmas service until the tree is removed.

11. Some Hay in a Manger

Aim

To bring the Christmas story alive for children and to lead them into worship.

Setting

Younger children's groups.

Equipment

Crib; straw; doll; crêpe bandages; other nativity props.

Outline

It is amazing how easy it is to lead very young children into worship if they have taken an active part in preparing for it. This is simply a telling of the Christmas story, but one that involves even the youngest of children. As you tell the story, invite the children to do the things Mary would have done for Jesus: put some clean straw in the crib, wrap him up in strips of cloth to keep him warm, and so on. Use your imagination as you tell the story, and find lots of active ways to involve the children.

You can then lead into some simple worship songs: you'll almost certainly find that the children will enter into this much more deeply than if you had approached it from cold, or from a telling of the story which didn't involve them as much.

It might be helpful to make up appropriate words to some of the songs that children sing at nursery. For example, to the tune of 'The Wheels on the Bus', sing:

The angels in the sky sang 'Praise you God'
'Praise you God'
'Praise you God'
The angels in the sky sang 'Praise you God
For our baby King'

The shepherds from the fields said 'Thank you God...
For our baby King'

All the children here sing 'Thank you God...
For our baby King'

Not quite Kendrick, but it does the trick, and it does lead into praise, unlike so many of the Christmas songs and hymns which simply tell the story and stop there!

New Year

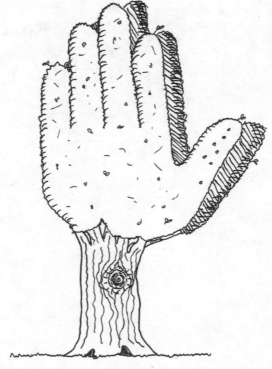

No. 12 'A Prayer Tree'

This event is not strictly in the church calendar, but it feels significant, and has gathered to itself a particular set of 'secular' customs, such as counting down to midnight, singing 'Auld Lang Syne', popping champagne corks, and so on. Many Christians prefer to give it a slightly more spiritual treatment, with a Watchnight service.

The sense of new beginnings is an important one at this time, and our continual making and breaking of resolutions demonstrates the desire deep within the human heart for something better, and also our complete failure to be able to make it happen. To keep Jesus at the centre of our New Year festivities, and to bring our prayers, hopes and dreams for the future to him in intercession, should be the aim of a truly Christian celebration.

12. A Prayer Tree

Aim

To help people to bring to God their hopes and prayers for the year ahead.

Setting

In church, or in the children's group room.

Equipment

Jesse Tree (see Outline No. 5); pens; green card cut out into leaf shapes, with cotton loops for hanging.

Outline

Remove all the pictures and models from the tree so that it is just bare sticks again. Encourage people to think and to listen to God about their hopes and dreams for the New Year just beginning, and to write a brief hope, dream or prayer onto a leaf-shaped piece of card. Adults will need to help very young children: the exercise may be done in small groups helping each other.

During a quiet time of prayer, perhaps with appropriate music in the background, people can be encouraged to come forward and hang their prayer-leaf on the tree, either silently or with a spoken prayer. This time can be ended by gathering together with a prayer led from the front, or an appropriate song.

13. Hasn't She Grown!

Aim

To give thanks for our growth in discipleship over the past year, and to look forward to what God is going to teach us in the year ahead.

Setting

Children's groups.

Equipment

Tell the children to bring along any photos they can get from their family of last Christmas, a year ago. Alternatively, find photos of summer holidays eighteen months ago, or school photos which are more than a year old.

Outline

Show each other your photos, and emphasise things like how much older they look now, how those clothes don't fit them any more, how they've now grown out of those toys, how their hair is different, how they've got new front teeth, or whatever.

Talk about how time moves on, and emphasise ways in which the last year has been a year of change, growth and new learning. Then encourage the children to talk about the things they've learnt about God over the past year, and ways in which they've experienced him and grown close to him. What have been the significant milestones? It really would be inappropriate to still be behaving/praying/understanding as they were a year ago.

Spend time giving thanks to God for all he's done over the past year, and pray that he'll continue to help us grow in our faith. Some kind of rededication activity might be appropriate to round off the session.

14. Hopes and Fears

Aim

To encourage the children to bring to God their hopes and fears for the year ahead.

Setting

Older children's groups, or possibly an all-age service.

Equipment

Large wooden cross which can stand up or be propped up; two rucksacks; bits of paper or card cut into the shape of walking boots; felt pens.

Outline

This idea is based around these lines from 'O Little Town of Bethlehem':

The hopes and fears of all the years
Are met in thee tonight.

Begin by talking about someone setting out on a long journey. Jesus and his parents running away to Egypt would be a good seasonal one (although try to avoid a long explanation of the reason for the flight, which is not the main point of this). Alternatively you could use the story of Abraham, or Jesus and the disciples going out on the lake in a boat, etc.

Build up some atmosphere by talking about how the people felt as they got ready to set out, what they might have packed for the journey, and so on. Then move on to talk about how they might have felt about the journey itself: what good things might happen, and what they might have been scared or worried about.

As we begin our journey into a new year, we too might have all sorts of things we're excited about, and probably some real fears and concerns too. Invite the children to take two bits of paper, and to write on one the thing they're most hopeful about or looking forward to in the year ahead (new school, special holiday, new baby brother or sister, etc.). On the other piece get them to write, if they'd like to, one thing they're worried about as they look ahead. Assure them that these fears will not be made public. This needs handling sensitively: children do have real fears, but are seldom invited to talk about them. However, the idea is not to put into them the fears of others which had never occurred to them!

Turning these hopes and fears into prayers can be handled in different ways. If your group is small enough, and time permits, each child could put their 'hope' piece of paper into one of the rucksacks, and say a prayer about it, perhaps asking God for it to come true, or praying for any other people it might involve. Alternatively, you could put all the papers in and then split into small groups for a few minutes of the children praying about their hopes. Finally, hang the rucksack on the cross as a sign of handing over our dreams to the will of Jesus.

The fears need to be handled in a different way: it is probably best to invite the children to put their 'fears' into the other rucksack in silence, and to hang that on the other side of the cross as a way of bringing them to Jesus for him to carry, sharing the burden as the children walk on into the future. A leader should offer to pray privately with any child about their fears, but should try to involve another child whom they consider suitable to pray with them, so that this is mutual ministry, and not just leaders doing it to the children.

Finally, each child can be given a third boot-shaped piece of paper or card to take home, with a verse on it such as 'I am with you always' (Matthew 28:20). A song such as 'Over all the earth (Reign in me again)' would round this session off suitably.

15. Instant Psalm

Aim

To create a Psalm celebrating God's presence during the past year.

Setting

Children's groups, with a possible 'performance' during an all-age service.

Equipment

Flipchart or OHP and pens; paper and paints for possible illustration later.

Outline

The Psalms were for centuries the songbook of God's people, but sadly they have become a neglected treasure for most Christians, simply because we're not quite sure how to use them. This idea allows you to create one of your own.

One category of Psalm is what the theologians call 'Recitals of Mighty Acts', where God is praised for the things he has done in the life of the individual or the nation. Psalms 78, 104, 105, 106 and 107, for example, fall into this category, but we're going to concentrate on Psalm 136, where a refrain is repeated, probably by the congregation, while a leader or cantor sings the first half of each verse.

The idea is to look back over the life of the church or group and identify some key events, stages or moments, both good and bad, and make them into a Psalm with a repeated refrain. You might like to use 'His love endures for ever', as Psalm 136 does, or you could think up a different response, such as 'You were with us' or 'The Lord cared for us'. New Year would be a good time to do this, or alternatively, if this is more the time when things get started in your church, in September when the schools go back. Perhaps you could use your Psalm to start off the church year on Advent Sunday.

Think with the children about some of the key events in the life of the group or the church, and collect them on a flipchart, possibly arranged on a time line. Then in pairs or small groups the children could each choose an event and make up a two-line verse about it, to fit with the refrain. Examples might be:

When we got more than we were aiming for
at our Gift Day
The Lord cared for us

When Sally broke her leg
and had to go into hospital
The Lord cared for us

When we all went
to Alton Towers
The Lord cared for us

Initially this could be used within the group as an act of worship, with everyone joining in the refrain and each individual or group contributing their verse, but you may then like to prepare for leading the whole church in worship by illustrating some of the key events and holding them up at the appropriate time, with the whole congregation joining in the refrain.

Epiphany

No. 16 'Gold, Frankincense and Myrrh'

This is the festival, celebrated on January 6th (the 'twelfth day of Christmas'), when we remember the visit of the Wise Men to Jesus, and their presentation of gifts to him. The colour is white or gold, and the story can be found in Matthew 2.

Originally, the festival had a completely different meaning. In the Eastern churches it was the two-fold celebration of the 'revealing' or 'shining out' (Greek *epiphaneia*) of Jesus, into the world at his birth, and into public ministry at his baptism. In the East this was *the* Christmas celebration, but as the Western celebration of December 25th as the birthday of Jesus spread, Epiphany became by the fourth century a different festival, with the Magi as the key figures. This led to the later emphasis of Jesus being revealed to, and worshipped by, those outside the Jewish faith and culture. The festival is now often linked with the worldwide mission of the church to reveal Jesus to everyone of every culture, working and praying towards that time when every knee from every nation on earth will bow before him.

Two other gospel themes are linked with Epiphany, both to do with new revelation and new beginnings. We have already mentioned the ancient link with the baptism of Jesus, which in the latest church calendar has a day of its own, on the Sunday after Epiphany. The third is the miracle at the wedding in Cana, when Jesus turned water into wine and first revealed his supernatural power. Because it is the first festival of the year, the theme of new beginnings is often linked with the 'secular' New Year.

16. Gold, Frankincense and Myrrh

Aim

To use the gifts brought by the Wise Men as prompts to renewing our own discipleship at the start of a new year.

Setting

Children's groups or all-age services.

Equipment

Gold, frankincense, myrrh (or equivalents!) and a crib scene.

Outline

Tell the story of the Wise Men's journey, and draw out the significance of their gifts as perhaps representing money/riches, worship and adoration, and preparation for the death of Jesus.

During the singing of a hymn or song, the whole congregation may be led in procession by three individuals of differing ages, carrying the gifts, which are then presented at and placed into the crib scene. When it comes to the incense, this can be more dramatic if a bowl of glowing charcoal is already in the crib, and grains of incense are sprinkled onto it. The resulting billows of smoke are most dramatic, and can speak of our praise and worship ascending to the throne of God. Ask a local high Anglican or Catholic church for help with incense if you're unfamiliar with its workings!

At each presentation, pause while the leader invites the Holy Spirit to come and stir people's hearts to respond in the appropriate way. Allow silence for him to speak to people, and then use a responsive prayer to draw things together and move you on.

Appropriate songs of offering or surrender, such as 'I will offer up my life', might complete this part of the service.

17. Shine, Jesus, Shine

Aim

To pray for the world.

Setting

All-age services. This could also be used at an adult prayer meeting or homegroup.

Equipment

Large map of the world, either a simple hand-drawn one or a proper printed one; tea-light candles.

Reading

John 8:12–18.

Outline

Talk about Jesus, the light of the world, and the different areas of the world which are in different kinds of darkness.

In family or other small groups, listen to God for him to put one particular geographical area or nation on your hearts, and then pray silently for that area by lighting a candle and placing it on that part of the map. Then use the map as a visual aid in praying for the world as a whole, either with corporate silence (not too long if young children are present), led intercessions, open prayer, or through song. 'Great is the darkness' or 'Shine, Jesus, shine' would be appropriate.

Leave the candles burning after the service is over and as people leave, reminding them that they should go on praying through the week.

18. Starry Sky

Aim

To allow the opportunity to rededicate ourselves to witness and evangelism.

Setting

Children's groups.

Equipment

Nativity scene on a large sheet of paper and put on a wall (possibly one you've made earlier as a group); cut-out stars made of card; sticky pads or Blu-tak; pens.

Outline

This idea has worked well with younger children. Tell the story of the star which led the Wise Men to find Jesus. Explain that we too can lead other people to Jesus so that they can become his friends, by telling them about him and how much he loves them, by the way we're kind to them, and so on.

Give each child a star, and get them to write their name on it, with help if necessary. Then, as an act of commitment to helping others find Jesus, get them to stick their stars in the sky over your crib scene, using sticky pads or Blu-tak. Pray together that Jesus will help us to help others to find him as their friends. A song like 'This little light of mine' (perhaps changed to 'This little star of mine' would round off this activity.

19. An Object Lesson

Aim

To allow children to understand, experience and praise God for different aspects of his character.

Setting

Children's groups.

Equipment

A crib scene of some description, and various objects which might represent different names, titles or attributes of God, for example a torch (light of the world), a map (guide), a toy doctor's kit (healer), a roll or slice of bread (bread of life), a toy lamb (shepherd) and so on. Get together as many as you can.

Outline

The Wise Men brought gifts to the baby Jesus which reflected something of his character and purpose in life: gold for a king, incense for a god, myrrh for a death. Explain that we are going to offer gifts of worship to Jesus in a way that picks up some of his other attributes or roles. Have the objects you've chosen on display, and invite the children to choose one that feels most appropriate for them now. Don't explain what each object represents, but let them speak to the children as the Holy Spirit allows. After each child has chosen something, they should reverently offer it to Jesus at the crib.

Invite them then to form into small groups, and to share, if they'd like to, which object they chose and why. Some of the choices may be pretty arbitrary, but others may have deep significance, and a leader with each group should help the children to be sensitive to one another as they listen.

The action can then be developed in two ways: you could move into a time of praise for the different aspects of God's character, using appropriate songs or prayers. But it may also be right to spend time ministering to one another, asking God to come to each child in a way related to the object they've chosen; for example to bring light to the darkness when they're afraid at night, to come to guide them about a decision they have to make, and so on.

This can be a very powerful way of ministering to both children and adults. Having prayed for God to come to them, wait for a while in silence and then ask what is happening for them. For instance, they may have seen a picture in their mind in which God will have brought what it was they wanted from him.

Pray finally for God to bless the child, and share any words or pictures which others in the group may have received for them.

The Baptism of Christ

No. 22 'Teddy Bears' Picnic'

Celebrated on the Sunday after the Epiphany, this occasion serves to remind us of the start of Jesus' ministry, his empowering by the Holy Spirit, and his approval from the Father. It can remind us of our own baptism (or help us to look forward to it), and it can act as a reminder in our often graceless and performance-driven society that we are accepted and loved by a Father who is well pleased with us *before* we've achieved anything, not afterwards.

Celebration of this festival can challenge us to recommit

ourselves to the promises we made or which were made for us at our baptism, and can provide a good opportunity for us to receive a refilling with the Holy Spirit, and new empowerment for ministry. It could also be an appropriate time, particularly as it falls close to the start of a new year, to commission people to new areas or new phases of ministry.

20. Say That Again

Aim

To renew baptism promises.

Equipment

Large (preferably unbreakable) bowls of water; branches of close-leaved trees or shrubs (conifers with needles or sprigs of rosemary work well).

Outline

Talk about the value of renewing promises, either because you've lapsed a bit from keeping them, or because you still mean what you said some time ago. Use some words which would have been used when people were baptised, and then invite people to make the appropriate responses. If you use liturgy in your church you can use the forms available for reaffirming baptismal promises; if not, a simple piece of liturgy such as this will do the trick:

In baptism God calls us out of darkness into his marvellous light. To follow Christ means dying to sin and rising to new life with him. Therefore I ask:

Do you reject the Devil and all rebellion against God?
I reject them.
Do you renounce the deceit and corruption of evil?

I renounce them.
Do you repent of the sins that separate us from God and neighbour?
I repent of them.
Do you turn to Christ as Saviour?
I turn to Christ.
Do you submit to Christ as Lord?
I submit to Christ.
Do you come to Christ the way, the truth and the life?
I come to Christ.

May God who has given you the desire to follow Christ give you strength to continue in the way. *Amen.*[1]

A few people, depending on the size of your church, should then be sent around the congregation with bowls and sprigs to sprinkle people with water. The leaves are dipped into the water and swished in the air above people's heads, with the words 'Remember your baptism into Christ' shouted loudly and joyfully. Children could be used to sprinkle people if a responsible adult carries their bowl for them: the sprinkling should be liberal without reaching the point of total saturation!

The presence of children, who will love feeling the drops of water hit them, will turn this from the rather solemn ritual practised in some churches into a genuinely joyous celebration of our baptism, and will give the grown-ups permission to enjoy it too.

NB: Non-paedo-baptist churches will need to adapt the wording used so that children can look forward to their baptism as well as adults looking back to theirs. But the sprinkling can still be as much fun!

---

[1] Taken from *Common Worship: Initiation Services* (Church House Publishing, 1998) pp. 106f.

21. Follow Me!

Aim

To call children into following Jesus, or to encourage them to move on in following him.

Setting

Children's groups.

Equipment

Inflatable dinghies are optional but could help if you can get hold of them.

Reading

Luke 5:1–11.

Outline

After his baptism, Jesus began to call those who would be his fellow-workers. This is an acting out of Jesus' call to the first disciples and to us, which emphasises the idea of leaving things behind. For baptised Christians, our baptism was a call to follow Jesus.

Get the children into groups, and sit them on the floor in their groups, roughly in the shape of a boat, or, if you've got them, sit them in the boats. A leader walks around them, telling the story of Jesus' calling of the first disciples from Luke 5:1–11. Telling it with your own elaborations will bring it to life much more than simply reading it from the Bible. At various points during the story the leader should pick a few individual children from the groups, who then get up and follow him/her around as the story continues.

When the story has ended, the leader should put the children who have been called safely on the 'shore', and talk about what following Jesus means. For example, the children had to get up and do something, they had to leave behind what they were doing and the people they were with, and they had to keep their eyes on the leader and go wherever they were led.

Invite stories from the children about what it actually means for them to be following Jesus, and about some of the things they have had to leave behind. Once you feel the points have been made, move into a ministry time, asking for initial or renewed commitment to following Jesus, empowering to stay close to him, and prayer for any who are finding it particularly difficult to walk with him at the moment. It may be that the leaving behind issue is important for some of the children.

You could use this idea along with a reaffirmation of baptism promises as in the previous idea.

22. Teddy Bears' Picnic

Aim

To help children realise how special they are to Jesus.

Setting

Younger children's groups.

Equipment

Toy cups and plates for a teddy bears' tea party, and squash and biscuits for the children.

Outline

The week before, ask the children to bring in their one very favourite teddy or other soft toy. Begin by getting the children to introduce their toy to the whole group, telling about its name, how long they've had it, where they take it, and so on. Draw out how special these creatures are to their owners.

Then go on to have a tea party for these most special friends, and afterwards a leader should tell the story of Jesus' baptism, concentrating especially on the Father's voice from heaven telling everyone how special Jesus was to him, not because he had achieved anything yet, but simply because he was his son.

As Jesus' brothers and sisters, we are special to God too, even more special than our teddies are to us. During some appropriate sung worship ('Lord Jesus I love you', 'Jesus' love is very wonderful', or 'Thank you Jesus') you could invite the Holy Spirit to come and bathe the children in the Father's love, letting them feel how special they are to him.

Candlemas

No. 23 'Character Trays'

Candlemas has, since the eighth century, been celebrated on February 2nd, although it was observed locally in Jerusalem from about AD 350. It officially brings to a close the Christmas season, and turns our attention towards the cross and Easter. It marks the gospel incident from Luke 2 when Jesus was presented in the temple, forty days after his birth, and was met by Anna and Simeon. It is about the fulfilment of long-awaited hopes, and as such it provides a turning point between past and future. The incident also symbolises the meeting of the Old Testament, represented by the aged prophet Simeon, and the new covenant which Jesus comes to inaugurate. Simeon can now 'depart in peace' as Jesus arrives on the stage of history.

It became traditional to give lighted candles to everyone at this service, to represent Jesus the Light of the World entering the darkness of human existence. At the end, everyone would turn physically towards the back of the church, and blow out their candles, turning from Christmas and looking towards the cross.

As Jesus was presented to God, so we can offer ourselves to his service.

23. Character Trays

Aim

To offer ourselves and all we are to Jesus.

Setting

All-age services or children's groups.

Equipment

Battered tin tray; guitar; CD player and CDs; Barbie doll; Playstation (or similar equivalents).

Outline

A leader should read out, or preferably tell, the following story, perhaps with previously prepared children acting it out.

The day of the toy service had arrived at last. The children had been preparing for it for weeks. Karen, the leader, had talked with the children about how fortunate they were to have all the toys and games and things that they just took for granted, when there were other children in their own city who didn't have very much at all. She had helped them to think about how God felt about this, and to ask him what he wanted each of them to give as a way of saying thank you for all that they had received from him.

The children had thought about it long and hard and were

really excited now that the day was here when they could give what they knew in their hearts God had asked of them. As they arrived at the service they looked at the presents the others had brought. Paul had a guitar which was very precious to him. Rachel had a personal CD player and some CDs, Edward had his Playstation and Vicki had her newest Barbie doll. It seemed as if everyone had brought their real treasures. That was until Anna walked in. She didn't have anything in her hands except a battered old tin tray. The others were puzzled. Paul sidled up to her. 'Haven't you remembered?' he whispered. 'It's the toy service today. You're supposed to have brought your best gift to give back to God.' 'I know,' said Anna. 'I have.'

There wasn't any chance to say any more as the service was starting. The children waited eagerly for the opportunity to present their gifts. Finally the vicar announced that the time had come for them to come forward. They formed an orderly procession, Paul with his guitar, Rachel with her personal CD player, Edward with his Playstation, Vicki with her Barbie doll and Anna with her tin tray. The minister took them and carefully laid each one at the foot of the cross. When Anna got to the front she carefully laid the tin tray down on the floor and stood on it. 'Here you are, Jesus,' she said. 'I give to you everything that is on this tray.'

Children can then be encouraged to make a personal response, either by going to stand briefly on the tray, or by placing on it a symbol of themselves, perhaps their 'face' from the next outline.

24. Face Forward

Aim

To offer ourselves and all we are to Jesus.

Setting

All-age services or children's groups.

Equipment

A4 sheets of paper each with a different face on, printed from a computer clip-art programme; felt pens.

Reading

Luke 2:22–38.

Outline

Print out a selection of different stylised or cartoon faces, chosen for their wide variation: boys, girls, all ages, long hair, short hair, no hair, glasses or not. . . .

At an appropriate point in the service invite people forward to select a face which looks a bit like them. You can give time in small groups to allow further customisation (adding a beard, or plaits) until each person has a reasonable picture of themselves.

You can then use these as symbols for the people, which

can be offered to God, just as Jesus was offered to him at the temple. They may be placed at the foot of a cross, or possibly on the tray from the previous activity.

You may want to use this self-offering as a time for personal prayer ministry: as each person presents themselves to Jesus, others may ask God for prophetic words of encouragement for them, just as Jesus was prophesied over by Anna.

25. Best Foot Forward

Aim

To give thanks for the milestones we have already passed in our journey of faith and to offer ourselves again to God for the future.

Setting

Older children's groups.

Equipment

Lots of big sheets of paper; rolls of lining paper or frieze paper; pens; scissors; CD and player; a focal point such as a cross.

Outline

Have everyone draw round one of their feet eight or ten times and cut the footprints out. Introduce the idea of life as a journey and talk about the different stages we go through on the way. Move on to talk about our Christian life in similar terms.

Ask either a leader or one of the children, who has previously been warned, to tell their story in a way which brings out milestones common to other members of the group. These could include things like being baptised as a baby, being brought to church, learning to pray out loud, choosing to pray as opposed to being asked to pray by a leader or parent, enjoying hearing stories about Jesus, their first communion, joining the group, speaking in tongues and so on. Continue by talking about everyone's story being different and identify some more milestones.

Then ask the group to think back over their own lives, identify the milestones on their own particular journey and write one on each of their footprints. One footprint, however, must remain blank for use later. Children should be encouraged to share something of their story with the rest of the group (or in smaller groups to save time), mounting their footprints on a long piece of paper as they go.

This could lead into a time of thanksgiving for God's hand upon their lives and for those who have been particularly significant in helping them on their journey. 'Come on and celebrate' or 'Great is the Lord and most worthy of praise' could be used, and people could be encouraged to speak out short prayers of thanks for what is past.

Finally this time could be rounded off with a look forward, and the opportunity to take the final footprint and place it at the foot of the cross as a way of rededicating ourselves to walking with God into the future. A song expressing this, such as 'I will offer up my life', could be played on CD, as people have some space to move about the room and worship without disturbing others too much.

Lent

No. 30 'Slavery to Freedom'

The season of Lent is one of the few Christian observances apart from Christmas and Easter that the person in the street would have some idea about, and most of it would be negative! It began as a memorial of the cross, since Good Friday would not have been kept as a separate event, but only Easter Eve and Easter Day. But by the mid fourth century it had become, along with Advent, a season of preparation before a major festival, and it became linked with Jesus' forty-day fast in the desert. It is a time to reflect on where we are with God, a time to resist sin even more stringently, a time of austerity and sacrifice, possibly marked by giving up something that is not in itself wrong but which might have too much of a hold on us for our spiritual health.

In the past, fat or oil would have been banned by the church during Lent (another example of how easy it is to turn helpful devotional exercises into set laws), so people would use up all their fat in making pancakes on the day before Lent started, a day when they would also go to confession to be forgiven (or 'shriven') for their sins. Ash Wednesday, the first day of Lent, is still marked in a growing number of churches with a service during which people have ash put on their foreheads – a reminder of the way people dealt with extreme sorrow for sin in the Old Testament.

In spite of all this, Lent need not be a miserable time, but it should be kept simple and austere, thus providing a dramatic contrast with the splendour of Easter Sunday. The liturgical colour is either purple or undyed sackcloth, and churches are often stripped of flowers or other decorations.

Since many of the ideas associated with Lent centre around confession and penitence, they may be used at any time of year as part of the normal period of reflection and penitence which should be one ingredient every time we gather to worship.

26. Dust and Ashes

Aim

To express our penitence to God.

Setting

Children's groups or an all-age service.

Equipment

Small bowls (stainless steel ice-cream dishes do nicely); ashes (burnt palm crosses or a crushed up charcoal block, with a few drops of water added); a slice of dry bread.

Outline

In the Old Testament when people reacted to conviction of sin or other bad news with deep sorrow, they would often express this by tearing their clothes and putting ash on their heads. See, for example, 2 Samuel 13:19; Esther 4:1, 3; Job 42:6; Isaiah 58:5.

For many centuries the church has used the first day of Lent as a time to focus on penitence for sin, and it became the custom, following the Old Testament practice, to put ash on the heads of the worshippers as an external sign of what was going on inside. The day became known as Ash Wednesday, and the 'imposition of ashes' is increasingly being used on that day in the contemporary church. For children, this might happen on the first Sunday in Lent.

Explain the Old Testament background as above, and invite the Holy Spirit to come and show particular areas which need attention, and to bring conviction and sorrow for those things. Children can then be invited to come and receive the ashes. This is normally done by the leader dipping the side of a thumb in the ash and water mixture, and making a small cross on the forehead of each child. The liturgical words used are not particularly child-friendly, so make up your own, such as 'Emma, may these ashes be a sign of the sadness you feel in your heart for disobeying God'. Suitable music could be played while this happens.

Far from being morbid and unhelpful for children, it provides an extremely healthy way of dealing with sin and guilt, which can set them free from all kinds of problems in later life. If only more adults could know deep sorrow for sin and the joy of receiving forgiveness.

You might like to close by reading some of Isaiah 61, and claiming the promise in verse 3 that God will give a crown instead of ashes. Children should be encouraged not to wipe the mark off their heads too quickly: this can provide a useful talking point later with their parents or other adults.

The fingers of those using the ashes are best cleaned by squeezing them into a slice of bread, and then washing with water.

27. Time to be Holy

Aim

To give more space during a prayer of confession for its impact to be increased.

Setting

Children's groups or all-age services.

Outline

In liturgical churches, like the Church of England, the prayers of confession come in three parts: the invitation, which focuses people and invites them to consider what they need to confess; the prayer of confession, when a set prayer is used to 'wrap up and deliver' to God the things we've been thinking about silently; and the absolution, when we are told by the leader that God does indeed forgive us if we have confessed meaningfully. The absolution rounds off and personalises our confession, and can at times be a very helpful and healing piece of ministry. But it can also make the whole process seem a bit too quick and easy.

Try spreading out the confession by interspersing spoken words with sung words and instrumental music: you might sing a song such as 'Lord, have mercy on us', then join in a prayer of confession, perhaps responsively (*Patterns for Worship* has plenty of suggestions) while the instruments continue to play quietly under the spoken words. You could then even sing your song again, before hearing the leader say an absolution or assurance of God's forgiveness, again as a voice-over.

Don't move too quickly to forgiveness: the idea is to allow a period of time to get in touch with the serious nature of sin.

Finally you could sing together another song such as 'O Lord, your tenderness' or 'Thank you for saving me'. The more smoothly and seamlessly your musicians can move from one song to another, without someone saying 'Now let's sing number . . .', the more the natural flow of the worship will be apparent.

28. All Stations

Aim

To prepare to walk with Jesus through the events of his passion, and to experience more deeply what it meant for him and means for us.

Setting

Children's groups, and then possibly an all-age service.

Equipment

Paper and felt pens, or modelling materials.

Outline

The 'Stations of the Cross' have a long history in the devotion of the Catholic Church, and you can see fourteen little plaques around the walls of many Anglican and Catholic churches. They represent different stages along the journey from Jesus' trial and condemnation, to his death and burial in the tomb. As an act of devotion, usually during Holy Week, but at other times of the year as well, people would move round the church from one station to the next, listening to read meditations and praying around each incident.

Unfortunately some of the fourteen 'stations' have more to do with legend than with Scripture; some are repeated (Jesus apparently fell over three times on the journey – you get the point after the first time!), and some may even be said to have descended into the realms of fanciful superstition. Nevertheless there is much of value here, and children can be made to own and take their place in the story by making the stations themselves.

Many books of prayers have meditations for the stations: Michel Quoist's classic *Prayers of Life* has some helpful ones. Select some of the more biblical incidents from the list (young children will probably cope with no more than six), and use them as aids to worship and prayer in your children's groups during the season of Lent. Talk about how Jesus might have felt, what other people involved felt, and try to apply it to our following of Jesus today. Listen carefully to the kinds of insights the children have, which may be very different from adult readings of the same story. Finally, each week, get the children to draw or model the incident, and to produce a picture or display which can then be placed around the church building.

On Good Friday use a child-friendly meditation, based on what you've heard as you've worked on the stations through Lent, to move round the stations, listening, praying and singing as you go.

Suggested stations for use with children would be:

1. Jesus is condemned to death
2. Jesus picks up his cross
3. Jesus falls for the first time
5. Simon of Cyrene helps to carry Jesus' cross
10. Jesus is stripped of his garments
12. Jesus is nailed to the cross
13. Jesus' body is given to his mother
14. Jesus is laid in the tomb

Don't be tempted to have Jesus rise from the dead to bring a happy ending: Easter Day is the time to celebrate resurrection. Of course we remember his death in the light of his resurrection, but to move on too quickly can rob us of helpful meditation on the cross and all it means to us.

29. Back to the Fold

Aim

To use an act of confession, emphasising that sin separates us not only from God but also from one another.

Setting

Younger children's groups.

Equipment

A small cut-out sheep for each child; a large green sheet of paper or card stuck onto a wall, with a picture stuck above it of Jesus holding a lamb.

Outline

This idea came from a friend who, while on a walk in the country through lots of fields of sheep, came across one field where there was a most awful racket going on. This turned out to be coming from a small pen in one corner of the field, where about twenty sheep had for some reason been separated from the rest, and were clearly not happy about it! The rest of the sheep in the open field were bleating loudly too.

My friend told this story, and explained that when we do things which are wrong it not only separates us from God but also cuts us off from one another, spoiling friendships and even creating longer-term feuds. Some ideas about how this happens were shared at child-friendly levels.

The children then moved into a time where they asked God to tell them about anything they had done which might have spoiled friendships with others. A simple prayer of confession was used, and then the children were invited, as a sign that they wanted to be back in fellowship with Jesus and other people, to stick their sheep onto the green 'field' close to where Jesus was standing. Then an absolution was used, assuring the children of Jesus' forgiveness and welcome home for them.

30. Slavery to Freedom

Aim

To teach that there are areas in our lives where we can be in slavery to sins and habits, but from which we can be set free.

Setting

Children's groups.

Equipment

Balloons (already blown up), one for each child; sticky labels; pens; string.

Readings

Exodus 14; John 8:34; Galatians 5:1.

Outline

Begin by telling or reminding the children of the story of the Exodus. The enslaved people of Israel were rescued by God and brought into the Promised Land: in the same way there are areas of our lives where we are in slavery, and from which God can release us into freedom.

Teach about some specific examples of recurring sins or habits appropriate to the age group of the children. Then invite the children to identify one area in their own life where they are in slavery to a particular sin or wrong habit. You should allow some quiet time for them to listen to God, and to invite him to show them any areas of slavery in their lives.

After a while, ask them to write whatever God has shown them onto a sticky label. They should then stick their label onto a previously inflated balloon, which they tie around one ankle like a ball and chain.

Suggest that the children try to move around the room with the balls and chains on their feet, as though they were very heavy weights. It helps the illusion if you ask them to try to keep their balloons on the floor. It can also help to have some background music: we used the relevant part of the sound-track from the *Prince of Egypt* CD.

Lead into a prayer of confession, and then get a leader to declare God's forgiveness, either by using a liturgical absolution such as that used in church, or simply by reading a Bible passage such as 1 John 1:8–9. As you join in the 'Amen' at the end of this, get the children to stamp on their balloons as a prophetic action symbolising God's forgiveness.

Lead on into a celebration of that forgiveness. You could include songs like 'Jesus we celebrate your victory', and then invite God to come and fill those present with power to live in this new freedom and not to be drawn back into slavery.

31. The Bridge to Life

Aim

To help the children to understand the work of the cross in bridging the gulf that sin created between people and God.

Setting

Children's groups.

Equipment

A large cross made out of paper or preferably fabric – the cross should be not much shorter than the length of your room; two large bits of paper (perhaps from a flipchart) with 'God' written on one and 'Us' on the other; strips of paper or cloth to make the other 'bridges', not long enough to bridge the gap between the two ends of the room (we used kitchen roll, but the reverse side of spare wallpaper would do); CD or tape player and ambient music.

Reading

Isaiah 59:1–3,12–16.

Outline

This evangelistic activity is an acting out by the children of the 'bridge to life' illustration of conversion. You will need a pretty large space for this to work properly. It is most effective to use the room lengthways in order to make the gulf between God and people as wide and unbridgeable as you can and to have a cross which is well able to bridge the gap, speaking of God being so much greater than the problem of sin.

Begin in the centre of the room with some lively sung worship during which you celebrate being together with one another in God's presence. Songs like 'Come on and celebrate' and 'Whether you're one or whether you're two' could usefully set the scene. Move on from this to teach or remind the children that this was how it was when God created the world: he meant people to walk and talk with him and to be his friends. Sadly people chose to go their own way and sin came into the world. This created a huge gulf between God and people since God cannot tolerate sin.

Move the children to one end of the room, and put a label representing God at the other end of the room with a big gap in between. Talk with the children about the sort of things people did that created that gap, and ask them to consider which of those things they do personally. Next talk about the fact that we were made to be friends with God and when people no longer had that friendship they began to try to find ways to bridge the gap and get to God again. As the children come up with suggestions write them on strips of paper, none of which are long enough to stretch the distance and bridge the gap.

Finally, explain that God in his mercy sent his son Jesus, and by dying on the cross and rising again he was able to take away all the sin and be the bridge across the gap. Place the paper or material in a cross shape between God and the children.

Tell the children that in a moment you are going to invite them to walk across the bridge. There could be a variety of things that this could mean to them. It could be a way of saying to God that they are sorry for going their own way and that they want to be his friend, or that even though they have said sorry before they still mean it, or all sorts of other things. Ask them to walk slowly, one at a time, perhaps talking quietly to God as they go, and encourage them to be quiet by playing some quiet worshipful music while this takes place.

Once everyone has done what they want to do, you could round off this section by leading a group confession and publicly giving assurance of God's forgiveness. Another sung worship time could follow, beginning quietly and meditatively before lightening a little. For example, 'I'm special' or 'Thank you for saving me' into 'Lord I lift your name on high' or 'What a wonderful Saviour is Jesus'. It might be a good idea to offer the chance for the children to talk to a leader at the end, if they feel the need to do so.

32. Flower Disarranging!

Aim

To bring home with fresh impact the destructive horror of sin.

Setting

Children's groups or all-age services.

Equipment

A single flower (carnations or roses work well).

Outline

The leader produces a flower, and talks for a couple of minutes about how wonderful and intricate it is, and invites people to consider the beauty of its colour, scent, petals and so on.

Then quite suddenly the leader grabs the flower head, rips it violently off, tears the petals up, throws them onto the floor and tramples on them. The shock value of this is used to tell people about how awful and destructive the human race is, and how God must feel when he sees the wonderful world he has created wilfully ruined.

While the immediate application of this illustration is ecological, it can be extended to broken relationships, missed opportunities, wilful disobedience, and so on.

This illustration will add a new depth to the prayers and

songs of penitence that follow. Songs might include 'Hear, O Lord, our cry', 'Great is the darkness' and 'Lord be in my mind'.

33. The Prodigal Son

Aim

To introduce children to the use of pictures as aids to worship.

Setting

Children's groups.

Equipment

Large poster of Rembrandt's *The Return of the Prodigal Son*; a copy of Henri Nouwen's book of the same name[1] will provide excellent background reading for leaders.

Reading

Luke 15:11–31.

Read the story of the Prodigal Son, and then explain that you're going to look at a picture which is just one person's depiction of the story. Show the picture, and allow the children to take it in. You can then deepen their interaction with it by asking leading questions, such as:

- Which bit of the story is this a picture of?

---

[1] H. Nouwen, *The Return of the Prodigal Son* (DLT, 1994).

- Who is who in the picture?
- How do you know that the son has run out of money?

Then move on to less factual questions like:
- How do you think the father/son is feeling?
- Which person do you think is the elder brother?
- How is he feeling?

Then begin to personalise it:
- Have you ever felt like the son/elder brother?
- How do you react when people say sorry to you?
- How does God the Father respond when you say sorry to him?

The use of the picture (or 'icon') can bring the story alive and help children to see themselves in it. The session could be rounded off with prayers or songs celebrating forgiveness and restoration.

Other pictures could be used in a similar way for other Bible stories or seasons, for example Rublev's icon of the Trinity or Holman Hunt's *Light of the World*.

34. Dirty Hands

Aim

To help children experience the fact that sin is against God and not just against other people.

Setting

Children's groups and all-age services.

Equipment

Sheets of newspaper (which allow ink to come off onto hands!); felt pens; bowls of water and soap; towels; large dustbin or rubbish bin.

Reading

Psalm 51.

Outline

Give each child a sheet of newspaper and tell them, 'We're going to use it as a way of confessing our sins.' They should write, in felt pen, one thing they are particularly ashamed of, which has hurt someone else. (These needn't be shared publicly!)

A leader should then tell the children they're forgiven, and as a sign they can throw their 'sins' away into the bin. Get them to screw up their newspaper as tightly as they can, and have fun aiming it into the bin.

Ask the children if they feel better, but then get them to look at their hands, which should be covered in newsprint. Explain that they are still dirty, even though they have heard human words of forgiveness. Encourage them to confess their sins to God in a time of silent or liturgical prayer. Get the children to wash their hands clean while you read other parts of Psalm 51, such as verses 7 to 12, and then use a prayer of absolution (declaring God's forgiveness) or a Bible reading such as 1 John 1:8–9. Songs such as 'Lord take away my sin' and 'God is the one who wants the best for me' could be used here to end this section with a celebration of what God has done.

Mothering Sunday

No. 36 'Come for Coffee'

The celebration of the fourth Sunday of Lent as Mothering Sunday or Mother's Day is a fairly late addition to the calendar, and its origins are hard to discover. The *Book of Common Prayer* Communion Service for this week would have included the reading of Galatians 4, where the church, or the 'Jerusalem which is above', is described as 'the mother of us all' (verse 26). We also know, although a cause-and-effect link with this reading is not provable, that this Sunday became both a time for people to visit the 'mother church' or cathedral of the diocese, and for girls in service to be given a day off to go home and visit their mothers, which suggests a dating for this custom not much earlier than Victorian times. Nowadays it is used to give thanks to God for our human mothers, and to treat them with cards, presents, and even breakfast in bed!

Note that in spite of its relatively late introduction, Mothering Sunday does have at least some Christian background, and can be celebrated thankfully and prayerfully. Father's Day, on the other hand, is a much more recent invention of the greetings card industry.

35. Heartfelt Thanks

Aim

To praise God for our mothers and to pray for them.

Setting

Children's groups.

Equipment

Coloured card (A4 folded to A5); heart shapes (just smaller than A5) cut out of coloured paper with 'Thanks Mum' written vertically down the left side; felt pens and glue. For younger children, a sheet suggesting helpful words beginning with the letters of 'THANKS MUM' should be provided, with, for example, 'terrific' or 'tremendous' in the 'T' section, and so on. This can take the emphasis off spelling and place it on praying. If you can get hold of one, a Hebrew Bible would be helpful.

Outline

Teach about the way Hebrew poets, when writing songs or poems of praise, would often write 'acrostics': each verse or group of verses beginning with the letters of the Hebrew alphabet. If you have a Bible, show them Psalm 119, where the verses of each eight-verse section begin with the same letter, in alphabetical order. This will also explain to inquisitive children why it says things like 'Aleph' and 'Heth' at the top of the sections – they are the names of the letters. Other acrostic Psalms, just for the record, are 9, 10, 25, 34, 37, 111, 112 and 145.

Give the children their paper hearts, and encourage them to make an acrostic poem of praise to their mums, by thinking of things they appreciate about them, for example:

T errific cook
H elpful and encouraging
A lways loving
N ice and cuddly
K ind and considerate
S pecial and loved

These hearts can then be used to encourage open prayers of thanks in the group, so that you can move on to pray for any particular needs mums might have. Finally stick the hearts onto the card for the children to take home.

It goes without saying that you may have to be sensitive towards children in the group whose experience of motherhood is less positive.

36. Come for Coffee

Aim

To say 'thank you' by practical acts of service.

Setting

Children's group and then after the service.

Equipment

Invitation cards; cooking ingredients; flowers and arranging materials; tablecloths; trays; tea; coffee; squash.

Outline

I've allocated this idea to Mother's Day, although that may not be the best occasion to do it, if people are rushing off to take their mums out to a proper lunch, for instance! You can use this idea any time you want to concentrate on practical service: for example, when it comes up in a reading or preaching/teaching theme. For a similar idea, more suitable for a youth group than for children, see the next Outline.

The General Thanksgiving, a piece of Anglican liturgy, talks about 'showing forth our praise not only with our lips but with our lives'. Explain that we're going to do that as a way of saying 'thank you' [to our mums] and sharing God's love with them.

Spend some time the week before, making and colouring

invitation cards, and then give them out as people leave church. On the week itself, spend time in the groups praying for the enterprise, asking that God will enable guests to feel welcomed and loved. Then groups can make simple cakes (Cornflake cakes, peppermint creams, etc.) and small flower arrangements as table decorations. Use tablecloths, and make your after-service coffee more special than usual. Get the children to act as waiters and waitresses, showing people to their seats and serving them.

37. Cocktails

Aim

To say 'thank you' by practical acts of service.

Setting

Older children's group and then after the service.

Equipment

Drinks; ice cream; sugar; egg white; fruit; large jugs; glasses (preferably plastic, but looking like glasses).

Outline

The idea is the same as the one above, but get the older children to create exotic non-alcoholic cocktails and think up names for them. These are then served to the congregation instead of coffee after the service, with the same concern for high quality, and the same emphasis on prayerful service.

Glasses may be frosted by dipping the rims in egg white and then castor sugar, but will need to be done in advance so that they dry. Your imagination is the limit: fruit juice or milkshake syrup can be added to fizzy drinks to flavour them, and little umbrellas or slices of orange used to make the drinks really special. Having said that, try not to make them too sickly!

This idea could also give a youth group a significant part in a shared church meal, Alpha supper or other social event.

38. Hidden Kindness

Aim

To give thanks for the many things mothers do for their children and to ask God to help children to bless their mothers.

Setting

Probably a younger children's group.

Equipment

Pictures (see below); Blu-tak; a flipchart with two columns drawn.

Outline

Before the session starts you will need several small pictures of mothers doing things for their children and of children doing things for their mothers. These can either be drawn as cartoon-style sketches, cut out from magazines or you might like to print out some computer clip-art.

Hide these pictures around the room in which you will be meeting. During the session ask the children to try to find all the pictures. When they have collected the pictures talk together about what is happening in each one, and as you do so stick them into one of two columns on the chart, depending on whether it is something Mum does for them or something they could do for Mum.

Have a time of prayer during which the children choose one of the pictures from each column. Encourage them to say a simple 'thank you' prayer relating to the 'Mum helping me' picture, and use the other picture to encourage them to ask God to help them do something kind or helpful for their mums.

Palm Sunday

No. 40 'Going Up to Worship'

The sixth Sunday of Lent, which begins Holy Week, is called Palm Sunday, because of the palm branches which were used by the crowd to welcome Jesus to Jerusalem, where he would face trial and death. Christians in Jerusalem, from the end of the fourth century, when they were no longer persecuted and could worship openly, would re-enact the triumphal entry of Jesus, meeting on the Sunday before Easter at the summit of the Mount of Olives and processing joyfully into the city. Children would have a special part to play in the celebrations. Gradually the observance spread, and became more stylised, since not many cities had Mounts of Olives to process down.

Palm Sunday is a time of joyful celebration of the kingship of Jesus, but the shadow of the cross falls over it all: Jesus is welcomed but later rejected, possibly by many of the same people. He weeps over the unbelieving city, and immediately

113

enters into conflict with the religious establishment as he throws the market traders out of the temple, and later the same week he is betrayed, denied and finally deserted by his friends. So Palm Sunday is a very rich and varied occasion to celebrate.

The gospel accounts of the triumphal entry include two points worth noting: Matthew tells us that children were at the forefront of those welcoming Jesus, and Luke adds creation itself: the very stones of the desert road would cry out in praise if the people were silenced.

The colour for Palm Sunday and Holy Week is red, looking forward to the blood of Jesus to be shed for us at the end of the week.

39. Palm Crosses

Aim

To use palm crosses in worship to welcome Jesus.

Setting

All-age services.

Equipment

Palm crosses, available from church supplies shops or by mail order from Charles Farris Ltd, Quarry Fields, Mere, Wilts BA12 6LA (0207 924 7544).

Reading

Matthew 21.

Outline

Palm crosses have been distributed in many churches on Palm Sunday as a visual aid in worship. There are various ways of doing this: people may be given a cross as they arrive, or they may be invited to come forward to get one at an appropriate point in the service. The crosses can then be held up or waved during songs or prayers, and they may be taken home and put up somewhere as a reminder of the passion of Jesus, or of some aspect of the story brought out in the preaching.

Traditionally they are burnt the following year on Ash Wednesday.

40. Going Up to Worship

Aim

To capture some of the excitement of the first Palm Sunday, and to consider the reactions of people in the crowd and invite people to respond to Jesus in a new way today.

Setting

All-age services or children's groups.

Equipment

Palm crosses; ribbons; banners.

Readings

Luke 19:28–40; Luke 23:13–25.

Outline

If possible gather the congregation in a different place a short distance from the normal worship area: for example, a church hall. You may need to warn them of this the week before and to have special arrangements for any who have mobility problems. As they arrive give everyone a palm cross, some other piece of greenery, a ribbon or a banner to help to create a carnival atmosphere and to wave later.

Begin with an explanation that on the first Palm Sunday the

people would have been going up to Jerusalem in joyful anticipation to celebrate the festival of Passover. They would
have been chatting and singing and greeting newcomers as
they journeyed, the throng getting ever bigger. Use an appropriate Psalm, for example Psalm 122, to shout antiphonally as
you process into the usual worship area, waving crosses, banners, etc. as you go. Go straight into a celebratory worship
time using appropriate songs like 'Jesus is the name we honour', 'We want to see Jesus lifted high', 'Blessed is the King
who comes' and 'Hosanna'. Include in this the reading
describing the events of the first Palm Sunday.

Use the second reading to identify the way that in five short
days the same people were shouting for Jesus' death. Base the
talk around three characters who could have been in the
crowd: Timid Tim, Frightened Fred and Lazy Laura. Paint
word pictures of these characters and the reasons why they
did not stick up for Jesus.

Timid Tim is the sort of person who hardly gets noticed in a
crowd; he likes to shrink into the background and not be the
focus of attention. He is happy to go along quietly with everybody else on Palm Sunday but on Good Friday he keeps very
very quiet indeed. He doesn't have the courage to stand up for
Jesus on his own, because he doesn't want to be different
from everybody else.

Frightened Fred, on the other hand, is a big beefy bully
type of person. He likes to be one of the lads. He is right in
the thick of it on Palm Sunday with the gang, leading the
cheering and encouraging others to join in too. But on Good
Friday the gang change their tune, and start shouting against
Jesus. He knows they are wrong and that he should be shouting *for* Jesus, but what would happen to him if he disagreed
with the gang? He is frightened. After all, they wouldn't want
him in the gang anymore; they might even turn and attack
him. It's better to keep quiet about what's right, keep your
head down and stay out of trouble!

Lastly there is Lazy Laura. She waves a palm on Palm

Sunday – a bit, between naps. She doesn't shout and praise but she really does (yawn) love Jesus. On Good Friday she hears what the crowd are all shouting, and knows they are wrong, but what is the point of disagreeing with them? She just can't be bothered, it is so tiring and who is going to listen to her anyway? So she says nothing.

After the talk, have a quiet time for people to think about their response to Jesus, and which of the characters they most identify with.

Lead into a prayer time which could include confession for failings and prayer for fresh empowering to stand strong for God, as well as intercession for others who have to stand up for what's right: for example, those in government, in authority, or in countries where people are persecuted for their faith. End with songs which will help people to express their response to God, such as 'Faithful one so unchanging' and 'I will offer up my life'. Invite people to take their palm crosses away with them and to use them as reminders during the week of the promises they may have made to God to take a stand for him.

41. The Way of the Cross

Aim

To help the children enter into the events of Holy Week and appreciate more fully Jesus' death for them.

Setting

Children's groups or possibly all-age services.

Equipment

See below.

Outline

The 'Stations of the Cross' (see Outline No. 28) are sometimes dramatised more fully as an act of open-air devotion which is a mix of worship, street theatre and meditation, with the 'congregation' playing the part of extras in the crowd and real actors and actresses taking the more major parts. This is a child-friendly 'Way of the Cross' which can be done during a single session. It should ideally be performed outdoors, in a churchyard or nearby garden, although if the weather is wet the church hall will do. The events are those of Holy Week rather than just Good Friday.

A leader tells the story, and then picks some children to act out each incident. For example, the preparations for the triumphal entry are done by two children going off to find a donkey (in fact a little toy on wheels), the cleansing of the temple involves someone tipping over a table loaded with all manner of furry creatures, and everything is watched by muttering 'Pharisees' dressed in robes.

The 'Last Supper' can allow time for refreshments and feet-washing, but try not to make the crucifixion too gruesome (although one little boy was really disappointed that his friend wasn't nailed up with real nails!).

Although this is meant to be fun, try to make it prayerful as well, and use worship songs as you move from one event to the next. 'Hosanna' or 'Blessed is the King who comes' will do for Palm Sunday, and more cross-centred songs might include 'Thank you Jesus' (without the resurrection verse), and 'Thank you for saving me'.

42. Feet First

Aim

To help the children to understand that we can worship God through the way we serve one another.

Setting

Children's groups.

Equipment

Large shallow containers; water; sand; gravel or little stones; clean compost; a huge piece of plastic or plenty of newspaper; several smaller bowls of water and towels; some cushions ready to be scattered on a clean part of the floor; some simple refreshments such as squash and biscuits.

Reading

John 13:1–17.

Outline

This is really a Maundy Thursday theme, but you could use it on Palm Sunday as an introduction to some of the events of Holy Week.

Start by asking everyone to take their shoes and socks off and roll up the bottoms of their trousers. Explain that today you are going to walk through the story as it is told. Begin the story by talking about Jesus and his disciples setting off on the journey to Jerusalem to celebrate the Passover there. Have everyone walk through the water first and then continue on the journey walking through the other containers as you carry on with the story, referring in passing to other events of Holy Week like the triumphal entry and particularly the preparations for the Last Supper. By the time your group arrives at the place where you are going to have your 'meal' they should have no lack of understanding as to why the disciples needed their feet washed!

Get everyone to sit round on the floor leaning on the cushions, and continue with the story up to and including the foot-washing. The leaders can then move among the children washing their feet for them before everyone enjoys the refreshments.

There are several ways that the session could develop from here. You could continue with the rest of the story of the Last Supper and remind the children of Jesus' first institution of communion. Or you could stay with the foot-washing and encourage the children to see that Jesus did this to show his disciples that they should show their love for God by the way they serve one another. This could lead into a prayerful time, giving thanks to Jesus for serving us and asking for his empowering to be like him.

Songs of worship that particularly fit include 'Jesus send me the helper', 'Make me a channel of your peace', 'I just want to live to please you (Take my life, Lord)' and 'The Servant King' (the verses of which are quite wordy, although the chorus could be used with even small children).

Good Friday

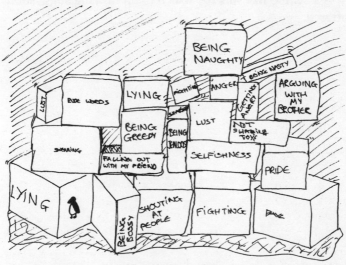

No. 43 'Demolition'

We have clear information from fourth-century Jerusalem of the way in which the Friday before Easter was celebrated. An all-night service in the Garden of Gethsemane would be followed by a procession to the city, where the gospel account of the trial of Jesus would be read. The people would move to pray at the pillar on which Jesus had been whipped. Then they could go home for a rest, gathering again in front of a piece of wood, supposedly from the cross, which the bishop set up in front of the crowd. They would pass by and kiss the wood, and then spend the three hours from noon to 3 p.m. listening to Scripture readings about the death of Jesus, its prediction in the Psalms and Prophets, and its interpretation in the Epistles.

At 3 p.m. the service would end, although many people would watch and pray all night.

These devotions are reflected in the practices of many churches today, with silent processions of witness in the morning, three hours of prayers and readings in the afternoon, and, in more Catholic churches, a service of 'Veneration of the Cross'. However, there is an increase in all-age services and it is a setting like this for which the following suggestions are offered.

43. Demolition

Aim

To show that our sins have caused a blockage between us and God but that when Jesus died on the cross to forgive us our sins he broke down the wall that separates us from him.

Setting

All-age services.

Equipment

A large cardboard box for everyone in the congregation. These are best collected in advance from friendly supermarkets and either painted white on one side (ordinary emulsion paint is fine) or covered in plain paper to hide any wording which could prove a distraction! You will also need one large felt pen for each person or family; a bed sheet (preferably close to the colour of the floor so as to be inconspicuous); and a cross.

Outline

In preparation, spread the sheet out on the floor at the front with a cross behind it, clearly visible.

Ask the congregation to identify the sorts of things that people do which don't please God, and which made it necessary for Jesus to go to the cross. If they are brave they may even identify things that they do!

Then give out the boxes and ask them to write just one of those things in large letters on their box. Young children may need help here but the ideas should still be theirs.

At some convenient point, possibly during the singing of a song, invite everyone to come and place their boxes at the front. A couple of people can then build a wall by placing the boxes on top of one another on the sheet. The wall should be as high as possible with the boxes arranged so that the words can be read by the congregation. With a medium-sized congregation, we managed to build a wall about three metres high and four metres wide. The cross, which is now behind the wall, is obscured from view, as are the two builders, who should crouch down out of sight.

Talk about the horrible things on the wall and how we have all done some of those things. You may wish to use some silence to allow God to speak to individuals about things they need to say sorry to him about before moving on to a time of confession. A responsive prayer could be good on this occasion as it would enable the non-readers to join in too.

After the confession the leader should then speak God's forgiveness to the congregation: as he/she does so the sheet can be pulled sharply out from under the wall by the two people behind it, causing it to tumble to the ground so that the cross is once more visible. The impact of this can be dramatic, and generally people will want to respond to God in praise and worship. The singing could begin with quieter songs which express the wonder of God's love for us, and then move on to more exuberant praise as appropriate, and perhaps give people the opportunity to recommit themselves to serving their loving God and Saviour.

Appropriate songs might include 'Amazing Love', 'Thank you for saving me', 'Jesus Christ (Once again)', 'I just want to live to please you (Take my life, Lord)' and 'Jesus touch me now'.

44. Hot Cross Buns

Aim

To encourage the children to revisit a familiar story in a different way and to respond again to Jesus' death on the cross for them.

Setting

At home or in children's groups.

Equipment

Enough hot cross buns for everyone.

Outline

Give each child a hot cross bun. Tell them, 'We can eat it in a few minutes, but first we are going to use it to help us meet with God.' While they are holding their buns, read the crucifixion story, preferably from a less gory children's Bible, and then invite them to find a space away from others where they can be alone for five minutes simply to look at the cross on their bun and allow the Holy Spirit to speak to them about Jesus' death for them. Encourage them to speak back to Jesus their response to him in the light of what they've been thinking about.

Then you can come back together, eat your buns, and join in with some worship songs such as 'Amazing Love', 'Thank you, Jesus', 'Thank you, Lord, for loving me' or 'I'm special'.

45. Caught Red-Handed

Aim

To drive home the fact that all of us are responsible for the death of Jesus.

Setting

All-age services or children's groups.

Equipment

Large cross of card (reinforced by wood); several large trays containing bright red water-based paint; bowls and towels for washing!

Outline

Make the point, either through a song or through teaching, that all of us have had a hand in the crucifixion of Jesus, through our sin.

Invite everyone to put a hand in the paint and place a handprint somewhere on the cross. This could be done in silence or with quiet ambient music. Invite people to consider anything particular in their own lives which their handprint might represent. When this is finished, you could use a song or liturgical prayer of confession. People can then wash their hands.

What is Jesus' response to our sin? Make a large sign with the words 'Father forgive' on it, and attach it to the cross, leaving it there for the rest of the service/group time.

46. Two Become One

Aim

To use the cross as a stimulus for praying for reconciliation.

Setting

All-age services or older children's groups.

Equipment

Six sets of three candles consisting of two smaller ones and one larger one, and something to stand them in or on. The smaller candles should be either side of the large one, and should be lit. The larger ones are unlit.

Reading

2 Corinthians 5:11–21.

Outline

This idea is based on the 'Marriage Candle' which is used at weddings to symbolise the bride and groom becoming one as a married couple. Here it is reapplied to a sometimes neglected nuance of the work of the cross: reconciliation. Spend some time thinking about the fact that in the cross pairs of opposites were brought together: sin and forgiveness, death and life, judgement and mercy, and so on.

In our world today there are all sorts of situations where reconciliation is needed: our prayer is that at the cross there can be healing. Brainstorm some situations where reconciliation is needed, or groups of people at enmity with each other. You might get Catholics and Protestants in Northern Ireland, Moslems and Christians in Sudan, black and white people in Britain, male and female, rich and poor people, and so on. You may also like to consider more personal issues: feuding halves of a family, parents recently separated or divorced, friends at school who have fallen out, or areas of tension and conflict within your own church or community.

Use the candles to bring these situations to the cross in prayer. Decide on a number of issues you want to pray about, and pair up the children (or adults), each representing one side of an issue. Each pair should come forward, mention briefly what they are representing, and pray for reconciliation by lighting the large central candle together from the two smaller ones. There can be a moment of quiet for the congregation to pray silently, and then a liturgical response could be used, such as

Lord Jesus, by your cross
Bring healing and peace. Amen.

NB: Don't blow out the smaller candles, but leave all three burning: reconciliation is not about the annihilation of differences, but bringing them together.

This act of prayer might end with a sharing of 'The Peace', whereby the congregation moves around freely exchanging greetings. The original idea for this was an opportunity for us to make sure we are at peace with each other before we approach God in worship. In this context, this act might have particular importance for any in the congregation who have issues between them.

47. Seeds of Hope 1

Aim

To help people to see afresh that just as Jesus had to die so we must let things which belong to our old life die in order that new fruit might grow.

Setting

The whole congregation at an all-age service.

Equipment

A couple of seed trays filled with clean seed compost (don't use real dirt from your garden because of the risk of contamination!); enough largish seeds for everyone, given out as they arrive (peas are quite good as they are large enough to get hold of individually).

Reading

John 12:24–26.

Outline

After teaching on this theme and text, invite people to listen to the Holy Spirit's prompting about things in their lives which need to die, so that something better can grow instead. Someone, for example, might have a problem with lying: they might want to put this to death so that truth can grow in their conversation.

Invite people to come forward, if they'd like to, and press their seed into the compost as a way of saying to God that they want whatever it represents to die, and that they are symbolically burying it in the earth. Prayers and/or songs of surrender and penitence could follow.

This should be followed up with Outline No. 53 in the Easter section.

Easter

No. 50 'Scrunchie Praise'

Easter is the single most important occasion in the Christian calendar, celebrating the resurrection of Jesus from the dead. Originally Easter would have spread over Saturday night and into Sunday, with the commemoration of both cross and resurrection, and was based around the Jewish Passover. But with the growth in importance of Good Friday in the fourth century, Easter Sunday itself became limited to the rising of Jesus.

Although not appropriate for this book, it is worth noting that Easter Eve has long had its own service, which would have included the baptism of new converts, and the restoring to the church's fellowship of those who had been under discipline and therefore separated from the worship of the church during Lent. While the *news* of the resurrection came to light on the Sunday morning, the resurrection itself happened at some unknown point during the night, so Christians have often celebrated Easter Eve as enthusiastically as Easter Day.

The whole mood of Easter contrasts sharply with the austerity and reflective nature of Holy Week, and many churches reflect this in their décor, with extravagant use of flowers and colour (white and gold are the liturgical colours). Chocolate is consumed in great quantities, not least by those who have fasted from it for the six weeks of Lent. Worship is celebratory, and liturgical churches use the response 'Alleluia! Christ is risen – He is risen indeed! Alleluia!' at the start of the service, echoing an early Christian greeting. Christians were not allowed to kneel to pray between Easter and Pentecost, and neither were they to fast on the Sundays following Easter.

The resurrection of Jesus looks forward to our resurrection from death, and assures us that not even death itself can separate us from the love of Christ.

48. Make Some Noise!

Aim

To celebrate the resurrection with as much noise as possible!

Setting

All-age services.

Equipment

Tell people the week before to bring to church anything they can find which will make a noise: party-squeakers, bells, gongs, noisy toys, etc. You will also need some flags, ribbons, banners and possibly sparklers.

Outline

An Easter Eve service would begin in darkness: at a particular point in the service the moment of resurrection itself (which happened at some point during the night) would be heralded with as much light, sound and movement as possible. You can begin your Easter morning service in a low-key way, and use some liturgy or a Bible reading to cue in a 'resurrection moment'.

Encourage people to keep their noise-making equipment as quiet as they can until you give your particular cue. Then they should go for it, with organists/musicians joining in and leading straight into a joyful song or hymn of resurrection. Many of the traditional Easter hymns are very child-friendly, with their repeated 'Alleluias'. Lights, flags and ribbons can be used to add a visual dimension to the aural one.

49. A Little More Noise

Aim

To encourage younger children to celebrate Easter with exuberant praise.

Setting

Younger children's groups, or a slot in an all-age service.

Equipment

Simple musical instruments and anything else with which young children can make a noise!

Outline

Following on from Outline No. 48, younger children too can be encouraged to celebrate the risen Jesus with noise. Tell them that they're going to praise Jesus by doing something they're all *really* good at: making a lot of noise. Give out the instruments, then count down three, two, one, GO! Everyone shouts, stamps their feet, and does whatever they do with their instruments. This will free the children to enter joyfully into sung worship, including 'God's not dead' and 'Why do you look here for the living?', perhaps leading into more subdued worship with 'I raise my hands up high' or 'Praise and glory to the name of Jesus'.

See the next Outline for a helpful way of loosening up young children physically in worship.

50. Scrunchie Praise

Aim

To help young children to express their worship using movement and their bodies.

Setting

Younger children's groups, or for young children in an all-age service.

Equipment

Hair scrunchies, each with a selection of coloured ribbons about 12 inches long sewn or tied onto them.

Outline

Very young children can worship with flags or ribbons, but they will tend to use a simple wrist movement to wave them backwards and forwards. By putting scrunchies around their wrists, you can encourage them to move much more freely, as they will need some quite dramatic arm movements to get the ribbons to fly.

This has the added advantage for young children that there are no sticks to poke in eyes!

51. The Easter Candle

Aim

To mark out the special time between the resurrection of Jesus and his ascension.

Setting

In church, or possibly in the children's group room.

Equipment

A very large candle, and somewhere safe and prominent to stand it.

Outline

In many churches the resurrection is hailed during the night or Easter Eve by the bringing into a dark church of a large lit candle, called the Easter or Paschal candle. This candle is then set up prominently and lit for every service between then and the Ascension.

The candle is traditionally blown out during the Ascension Day service (or you could do it on the following Sunday to involve children), but it is lit again throughout the year for baptisms, linking the baptism of the candidates with the death and resurrection of Jesus.

In some churches the candle is marked with the year and Alpha and Omega signs, showing Jesus as the Lord of all time, and with five nails, representing the wounds of the risen Lord.

52. What Comes Out ...

Aim

To teach the truth that since Christ was raised from the dead, he cannot die again (Romans 6:9).

Setting

Children's groups or an all-age service.

Equipment

A large onion; an amaryllis or hyacinth in full flower (you need to plan ahead for this one!); a hard-boiled egg; a party-popper.

Outline

Talk to the children about what the onion (which is *really* a bulb!), the egg and the party-popper all have in common: they've all got something inside them which, once it comes out, you can never get back inside again. The bulb will grow into the large dramatic flower (you may like to produce a hammer and pretend to attempt to get it back inside the bulb again).

The egg (with which you can scare people by throwing it around: if it does get dropped you can then say 'Good job I hard-boiled it first!') can't be put back together again once it's opened (you could get your musicians to play 'Humpty

Dumpty' in the background during this bit). And the party-popper, which you can let off, contains a 'pop' which can never be put back again.

You can then talk about Romans 6:9, and make the point that you can no more get Jesus back into the grave than you can get the pop back into the popper, and so on. Our Jesus is alive and with us for evermore! Encourage the children to speak out prayers of thanks and praise for Jesus' resurrection, and sing something like 'Jesus we celebrate your victory', 'Jesus isn't dead anymore' or 'He has risen!' (the chorus only for younger children).

53. Seeds of Hope 2

Aim

To complete the teaching about dying and bearing fruit, as a follow-up to Outline No. 47 on Good Friday.

Setting

The whole congregation at an all-age service.

Reading

John 12:24–26.

Outline

Tell/remind everyone about what you did on Good Friday with the seeds. At an opportune moment, produce seed trays the same as those you used before, but with sprouting new plants clearly visible (here's one I prepared earlier!). Use this to reinforce Jesus' promise of new life and fruit to be produced in us if we surrender our sins to him.

Celebrate together in worship the signs of new spiritual growth you can see around you, perhaps with testimonies or stories of growth. Songs along the lines of 'I am a new creation' and 'Great is the Lord and most worthy of praise' could be helpful.

54. Action Creed

Aim

To involve our bodies in worship in an accessible and unembarrassing way.

Setting

Primarily all-age worship.

Outline

Since the earliest years Christians have been proud to voice their beliefs in worship, in celebration of the truth, as acts of defiance in times of persecution, and to affirm biblical orthodoxy in times when it is under attack. These statements of belief are called 'creeds' (from the Latin for 'I believe'), and one of the earliest creeds we have is in Philippians 2:5–11. Like many other similar biblical passages, this passage would almost certainly have been learned by heart and recited during worship services. One piece of more recent Anglican liturgy which does the same job, and which has been widely used in many churches, is the acclamation

Christ has died,
Christ is risen,
Christ will come again!

A simple set of actions can bring this piece of liturgy alive in a way that does not feel as embarrassing as 'doing the actions to songs' can to those who find physical worship difficult.

The actions are these:

'Christ has died'	Extend arms as if on a cross, head down.
'Christ is risen'	Bring hands together and clap on the first syllable of 'risen'.
'Christ will come again'	Raise arms and look up.

This can then be repeated as the refrain for a responsive creed or affirmation of faith, as a response to prayers of intercession, or as a chant during a march or procession of witness. Easter would be a good time to use this idea, but of course it works throughout the year, except possibly during Lent.

Having grasped the principle, why not make up your own simple actions to other bits of liturgy which you use regularly, for example the Lord's Prayer?[1]

---

[1] See John Leach, *Living Liturgy* (Kingsway, 1997) p. 41 for further details of biblical liturgy.

Ascension

No. 55 'The Royal Family'

Ascension Day itself falls on the Thursday forty days after Easter and ten days before Pentecost, but most churches will pick up the theme on the following Sunday. Acts 1 tells of the final encounter of Jesus with his disciples before he was taken up into heaven, leaving the dual promise of the gift of the Holy Spirit and his return at the end of time. Originally Pentecost was the dual celebration of the ascent of Christ and the descent of the Holy Spirit, but the two became separated sometime between the fourth and ninth centuries.

There are two main themes around the ascension: that of waiting for the Spirit and that of the ascended Jesus returning to his rightful place in heaven to reign until that time when his faithful people will join him for ever. We worship Jesus 'risen, ascended, glorified', but we worship him with a longing for his power for our ministry now and for our face-to-face meeting when time has ended.

Many of the ideas below could equally well be used for the feast of Christ the King, just before Advent, but there is a subtle difference. Ascension is about Jesus in heaven praying for us, egging us on until our part of the race is finished, whereas Christ the King is more about the final reign of Jesus when this world will have been wound up for ever.

The other theme which Ascension celebrates is the continuing humanity of Jesus, even though he is now in heaven. It is easy to think of Jesus becoming human for thirty-three years and then returning to divinity, but this is a heresy called 'modalism' by the early church. Jesus remains human, and has taken our humanity up into heaven with him. The letter to the Hebrews explores this theme and the way it can encourage us now.

55. The Royal Family

Aim

To help children realise the fact that they are to reign with Jesus, and to experience the anointing of the Holy Spirit now.

Setting

Children's groups, or possibly an all-age service.

Equipment

Oil for anointing; tissues.

Outline

Talk about how in Old Testament times a new king would be anointed with oil as a sign both of his accession to the throne (often in the future) and of the need for the anointing of the Holy Spirit. See for example the anointing of David in 1 Samuel 16.

At the ascension, Jesus took our humanity into heaven with him, and promised that one day we would reign as kings and queens with him. Encourage children (and adults) to pray for one another, asking the Holy Spirit to equip them now to live as the royal family they will become, and then anoint one another with oil.

There are two ways of doing this: the safe churchy way and the proper messy way! The oil used is normally olive oil, which you can get from a supermarket, or, if you're fussy about it having been 'blessed' by a bishop, from your cathedral. It can be nice to mix a few drops of scented oil in with it.

The safe way is to dip a finger into the oil and smear it on the forehead of the person you're praying for, with a spoken prayer asking for the Holy Spirit to come to anoint them. The oil is often applied in the sign of the cross, and hands as well as head may be anointed. The proper way is to pour oil over the head so that it trickles down, but you may have some less-than-happy parents if you go for this method!

This type of prayer can be very powerful, and it is wise to have someone to catch people in case they rest in the Spirit: this is not uncommon!

Prayer with anointing can be used in other situations, for example for healing or after baptism to pray for baptism in the Holy Spirit.

56. Worship His Majesty

Aim

To celebrate Jesus ascending to his throne in heaven and to re-emphasise that Jesus our friend is also Jesus the King of kings.

Setting

The whole congregation.

Equipment

See below.

Outline

Before the service try to create a stunning sense of the glory of heaven by decorating the church with gold and other precious-looking fabrics, objects, etc. For example, use gold material, gold flower arrangements, golden communion vessels and vestments (if you possess them!) and even incense. If your building allows it, you could create an ante-room where people could wait beforehand for their audience with the King. They could perhaps be invited by the service leader to enter, and as they come into the worship area you could use some majestic, regal music such as the 'Hallelujah Chorus', 'Zadok the Priest', or Vaughan Williams' 'Old Hundredth' played loudly on CD.

In the worship aim not to be so 'familiar' with Jesus our friend as perhaps we can be on other occasions, but rather to come humbly and reverently into the presence of the King. Invite people to kneel to pray, especially if it is not normally your custom to do so (remembering, of course, to be sensitive to those who cannot physically kneel).

Songs speaking of the majesty of God could be used such as 'Majesty', 'Welcome King of kings', 'Jesus we enthrone you', 'We bow down' and others in a similar vein.

57. Jigsaw Praise

Aim

To encourage everyone to bring to a praise time their own particular experiences of Jesus.

Setting

Children's groups or all-age services.

Equipment

Large sheet of material, at least A1 size; length of dowelling or broom handle; sheet of coloured card; double-sided adhesive tape; felt pens; scissors.

Outline

This activity involves the children in assembling a banner for use in worship. Before the session, hem the material and provide the means to hang it up, perhaps with a piece of dowelling through a hem at the top. Cut out from the card a large crown shape which will cover a significant proportion of the cloth. Position the crown onto the cloth and draw around it. Then cut the card into pieces like a jigsaw: the number and age of your children will decide how complex the puzzle is, and how many pieces it has.

Draw onto the cloth the outline of each piece of the crown in its correct position, and number the back of each piece of card and its corresponding gap on the cloth. Finally stick a small piece of double-sided tape onto each bit of card, leaving the second bit of peel-off backing in place. Then hide the pieces of card around the room.

During the service explain that when we worship Jesus we each bring something to contribute, and that only together can we give King Jesus the worship he deserves: not one of us can grasp or express fully the whole of his glory individually. Send the children off on a treasure hunt to find the bits of coloured card, which can be attached one by one to the spaces on the cloth (the numbers providing the key) using the other side of the adhesive tape, until the full crown is completed. Together you have made the full picture.

Ask the children (and adults) to consider what they value most about King Jesus, and for what they would most like to worship him. They might like to share some of these thoughts in the whole group or in smaller groups. You can then go into a period of singing and praying, while your banner is paraded or displayed during the worship.

If you are working in a larger group, you might like to use the following variations. Add the word 'Jesus' or a title such as 'King of kings' to your banner: more jigsaw pieces can be made in exactly the same way as you have made pieces from the crown. Or you could make more than one banner, in which case the card would need to be of different colours, so you could identify to which picture each piece belonged.

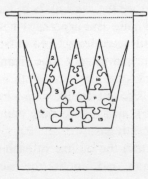

58. Egging Us On

Aim

To encourage children to persevere in discipleship, knowing that they have the intercession of Jesus himself to help them.

Setting

Children's groups.

Equipment

Two eggs (hard-boiled is safer!); a spoon for each child.

Reading

Hebrews 11–12.

Outline

Divide the children into two teams, and set up a relay race course, preferably of some length (go outside if your geography and the weather permits). At the winning post have two leaders, one for each team.

When the race starts, one leader sits at the end of the course totally uninterested, perhaps reading the paper, while the other constantly encourages the team, calling them on, rooting for them loudly and enthusiastically, and never in any way negatively.

At the end of the race, talk about how the teams felt as they were running, and how they felt about their leader's encouragement or lack of it. Talk about Jesus' encouragement of us in the race we run in real life (Hebrews 12:1–2), and how we can help one another to run to win.

Songs of commitment and perseverance could help to bring this message home, and you could spend time praying for any children who are facing difficult circumstances at the moment, or finding it hard to keep going.

59. Reflected Glory

Aim

To help children appreciate the glory of God which one day we will see for ourselves.

Setting

Children's groups.

Equipment

Flowers; candles; pretty stones; shells and other shiny objects; large mirrors.

Outline

Make an arrangement with the flowers and other objects (ensuring that the flower arrangement is circular and doesn't have a 'back'), and talk about how God's glory is shown through all these created things.

Then place three or more large mirrors behind the display, and notice how much more beauty and glory there is. Talk about the time when we shall see God in all his glory, not just the one-dimensional way we see things now. Use songs of worship to praise God for his glory.

60. Crowned with Glory Now

Aim

To worship Jesus risen, ascended and glorified, in contrast with the dying Saviour of Good Friday.

Setting

Younger children's groups.

Equipment

Large crown of thorns (barbed wire makes a very effective modern equivalent); chicken wire and oasis; fresh flowers.

Outline

You can begin with a useful recap of the story of Good Friday and Easter, making the point particularly that Jesus was crowned with a crown of thorns as an act of mockery. Tell again the story of the resurrection, and talk about how Jesus ascended to heaven and is now crowned as King of kings. Describe how 'today we're going to make him a much nicer crown as we bring our worship to him'.

Use the chicken wire and oasis to form a circular framework, and invite the children to select flowers and stick them in to make a beautiful floral crown. Encourage them to see each flower they use as a prayer of worship: they may even like to say brief prayers out loud.

Songs along the lines of 'Lord I lift your name on high' would provide suitable worship.

Pentecost

No. 67 'Light the Fire Again'

The Day of Pentecost in the Jewish calendar was the time of the first fruits of the harvest, when a few of the early crops would be cut and celebrated as a down-payment of God's goodness in bringing the full harvest later. Acts 2 tells the story of the Jews gathered in Jerusalem to celebrate the feast, when they were amazed suddenly to find a group of people bursting onto the street from a nearby house, proclaiming the wonderful deeds of God in many different languages. Peter stood up to preach about Jesus, and 3,000 people were converted as the first fruits of the church, which went on to traverse the globe. Pentecost is still celebrated as the birthday of the church.

Some Christians have been quick to see the contrast between Law and Spirit, and see in the wind and fire of Pentecost a backward glimpse to Mount Sinai, where God gave the Law to Moses. Just as the Israelites were unified into the Old Testament people of God through the giving of the Law, so the New Testament church was brought into being through the gift of the Spirit.

Churches today celebrate Pentecost as the main festival of the Holy Spirit and the birthday of the church: charismatic churches often use it as a particular focus for praying for people to be filled with the Spirit. The fire with which the first disciples were anointed is reflected in the liturgical colour of red.

61. Dressing Up

Aim

To encourage the congregation, including children, to enter into the celebration of this and other major festivals in the church's year.

Setting

All-age services.

Outline

The week before, ask everyone to come to church the following week wearing something bright red. The church has traditionally used different colours to represent different seasons: red speaks of the flames of fire at Pentecost when the Spirit came on the first disciples, and fire is a good symbol for the growth of the church around the world, encroaching upon and dispelling darkness and sin.

If your church does go in for liturgical colours, you could do the same thing at other times: purple on Advent Sunday, gold for Easter and Christmas, and so on. If you don't normally use colours, try it: you might enjoy it!

62. Happy Birthday, Dear Church

Aim

To join in birthday celebrations for the church.

Setting

Children's groups or possibly an all-age service.

Equipment

Large birthday cake.

Outline

Hold a birthday party for the church on its anniversary, with a cake, candles and so on.

Develop the theme by talking about the birth of the early church in Acts, and what it means to belong to the 'body of Christ'. Thank God for the gift of his church, and for the privilege of being called into it.

63. Feeling the Draught

Aim

To allow the children to receive the ministry of the Holy Spirit through the symbol of wind.

Setting

Children's groups.

Equipment

Play parachute.

Outline

Spend some time playing different games with the parachute, and lead into the fact that as the children move it about they can feel the breeze on their faces, legs, etc. Experiment with making soft gentle breezes and violent winds.

Talk about the biblical use of wind as a symbol for the Holy Spirit (in Hebrew the same word, *ruach*, means both). Tell the children that you're going to allow them to feel the breeze on their bodies, and that they can use the feeling to imagine the Holy Spirit coming to them to bless them, anoint or comfort them, or otherwise minister to them.

Get all the children to lie still on the floor while the leaders gently waft the parachute over them. One of the leaders should pray for the Holy Spirit to come and touch the children, just as they can feel the breeze of the parachute. Encourage the children to be open to the Spirit, and to listen for anything God might be saying to them.

This may sound contrived, but in my experience it can open the children up to a powerful touch from the Holy Spirit. For smaller children particularly, the physical feeling of the breeze can focus their attention long enough for them to receive from the Spirit. Try to avoid any sense that you are ministering to people by blowing on or fanning them: it is the Spirit who touches people, and the physical breeze is simply there to focus attention.

64. Pass the Parcel

Aim

To experience the gift of the Spirit as the one who himself gives gifts.

Setting

Children's groups.

Equipment

A parcel for passing, with smaller gifts individually wrapped and put between the layers of paper in the parcel; CD or tape player, or a live musician.

Outline

Talk about the Holy Spirit as the gift from God who himself comes to give gifts. Then get the children to unwrap their individual gifts (having carefully controlled the music so that each child has got one!) and talk about the need for them to unwrap and use the gifts the Spirit brings to them.

Move into a time of ministry and ask the Holy Spirit to come to bring his gifts to the children.

65. Speaking in Tongues

Aim

To allow children (and adults) to experience the gift of tongues.

Setting

Children's groups.

Reading

Acts 2.

Outline

Teach about the Holy Spirit's coming on the Day of Pentecost, and explain about the gift of tongues. You may like to refer to other New Testament passages, but keep it short and light.

Tell the children that the gift is still available today, and ask if any would like to share their experience of the gift, or to receive it if they haven't done so. Pray for them to receive the gift. If you're not used to this in your church, my book *Children's Ministry and the Holy Spirit*[1] takes you through a tried and tested process.

Move into a time of sung worship, which might include the use of singing in tongues, or making up words of praise in English to the tune being sung.

---

[1] Chris Leach, *Children's Ministry and the Holy Spirit* (Kingsway Publications, 2001).

66. The Spirit at Work

Aim

To encourage the children (and adults) to see the Holy Spirit at work in themselves and each other.

Setting

Children's groups, or possibly an all-age service.

Outline

Encourage the children to look around them, either through the windows or preferably by taking a short walk outside, to see the effects of the wind (trees moving, smoke blowing, washing on lines flapping etc.). They can't see the wind, but they can see what it does.

We can't see the Holy Spirit either, but we can see what he does. Talk about the gifts and fruit of the Spirit, the effects of the Spirit on people's lives, and put the children into small groups to talk about how they see the work of the Spirit in each other's lives. Encourage them to be encouraging, and then pray and give thanks for what the Spirit is doing among you. Finally you could pray for one another to be refilled with the Spirit so that his work can continue and grow.

67. Light the Fire Again

Aim

To develop an awareness that sin can quench the Holy Spirit, and to ask for and receive forgiveness.

Setting

Older children's groups, or possibly an all-age service.

Equipment

Candles with cardboard discs round, enough for one for each person. You can buy proper baptism candles, which have cardboard discs round them to stop any drips, from church suppliers, or you can make your own. One large candle, possibly the Easter candle (see Outline No. 51), should be lit and placed at the front.

Outline

Talk about the fact that although all Christians have received the Holy Spirit, the way in which we live can either enable him to work within us, or prevent it. Give each person a candle, and light them from the Easter candle or from one another. There is no symbolic significance at this stage: you simply need the candles to be lit! You can, however, make the link with the coming of the Spirit at Pentecost in flames of fire.

Talk about things we may have done to quench the Holy

Spirit or the gifts he may be wanting to give to us to use, and ask God to come and speak to people individually to identify specific things in their own lives. As God speaks to people, they should blow out their candles.

A prayer of corporate confession can be used by all at this point, after which prayer for refilling with the Spirit is appropriate, preferably in small groups or with one another. When everyone has received prayer, they should go and relight their candles from the central large candle, which has kept burning all through. This act is symbolic, and should be done in quiet reverence. Prayer or songs of rededication could follow, for example 'Don't let my love grow cold', 'Spirit of the living God', 'Jesus touch me now' or 'I just want to live to please you (Take my life, Lord)'.

68. Flowers in the Desert

Aim

To experience the refreshing and renewing power of the Holy Spirit.

Setting

Older children's groups, or an all-age service.

Equipment

Large bowl of dry sand, preferably quite coarse, and including some small bits of gravel; water; tree branches for sprinkling (see Outline No. 20); a flower for each person.

Reading

Isaiah 35.

Outline

Children may not relate instantly to the term 'spiritual dryness', but you ought to be able to tease out some discussion about those times when we feel less close to God, when living for him feels like hard work, when we don't feel our prayers are getting through, and so on. Talk about the way the Old Testament prophets sometimes used the image of the desert to describe these times. Talk about how a desert experience might feel, perhaps with the aid of some visuals and music (see Outline Nos. 76 and 77).

Invite any children who'd like to to come and run their hands through the sand, feeling its dryness and coarseness, and encourage them to make the link between these physical feelings and their inner spiritual state.

So often we feel that it's up to us to get ourselves sorted out when we're out of sorts with God: the story of redemption and the grace of God tell us the opposite. He delights to come to us when we have run out of resources, rather than demanding we somehow do it ourselves. Sprinkle water over the children as you make this point, and pray for the refreshing streams of the Holy Spirit to be released on them.

Finally give each child a flower, linking it back to the Isaiah reading, as a sign of God's promise of restoration and renewal.

This idea could be used at other times of the year, and possibly in conjunction with a reaffirming of baptism (see Outline No. 20). A similar activity, which makes the same point, but is limited to autumn time, is to use crispy dead leaves and to replace them with evergreens.

Trinity Sunday

No. 70 'The Writing's on the Wall'

Trinity Sunday does not commemorate an event from the life of Jesus, but rather the later theological understanding that God revealed himself as three persons yet one God. It was a latecomer in liturgical history, appearing at first in the tenth century, and only really gaining acceptance in the fourteenth. This Sunday, one week after Pentecost, is the bane of preachers' lives as they have to explain (again) all about the doctrine of the Trinity. Children won't grasp the finer points of theology, any more than the adults will actually, but if they are told simply that God is Father, Son and Holy Spirit they should be able to understand without asking too many awkward questions.

The doctrine of the Trinity can be broadened out with children to allow you to explore the multi-faceted character of God. This may take a while, but since the next twenty-odd

Sundays are known as 'Sundays after Trinity' in the church calendar, you won't be short of time to explore this theme if you choose to!

69. Trinity Leaves

Aim

To introduce the idea of God as three-in-one.

Setting

Families or children's groups, particularly for very young children.

Equipment

A clover patch.

Outline

Take the children to somewhere where there is a clover patch, and encourage them to pick a leaf each. Talk about how each leaf is a single leaf but is in three parts: that's how God is, as Father, Son and Holy Spirit. (Our four-year-old now always calls clover 'trinity leaves', and has even used the ones growing in the nursery garden to witness to her friends!)

You might like to worship using a simple liturgical creed: you can find a variety in *Patterns for Worship*, pp. 57 ff. You can also use some trinitarian songs such as 'Father we love you', or 'We worship you, Father, Son and Holy Spirit'.

70. The Writing's on the Wall

Aim

To help children to worship God through a wide variety of names and titles.

Setting

Children's groups.

Equipment

A roll of wallpaper with a brick pattern (alternatively paint a brick wall design beforehand); red and blue water-based paint and thick school-type paintbrushes.

Outline

Cut the wallpaper to fit a large noticeboard or wall where it can later be displayed. Spread it out on the floor or on long tables, and paint the word 'GOD' in the centre in very large letters.

Invite the children to brainstorm other names or titles for God, and then to paint them on, graffiti-style, all around the central word. When your wall is almost full up, and the paint dry enough not to run too much (a few runs will add authenticity to the graffiti look), fix it onto one wall of the room you're in.

During a period of sung worship the children could be

invited to quieten down and spend a few moments looking at the graffiti wall. They could ask the Holy Spirit to highlight one name of God that is particularly special to them at the moment, and/or you could invite them to share their personal experiences of God as healer, Father, etc.

The children can then offer prayers of thanks and worship to God, personalising and using some of the titles on the wall ('Thank you, God, that you are my best friend' or '... the one who comforts me when I'm feeling sad').

A final word of encouragement not to try this on the walls at home might be in order!

71. Graffiti Intercessions

Aim

To intercede for those in need, using the graffiti wall in Outline No. 70 and engaging our imaginations.

Setting

Children's groups or all-age services.

Equipment

Graffiti wall made in Outline No. 70, fixed up where it can be easily seen.

Outline

If you are transferring your wall painting into the church after having made it in your group, someone might like to explain to the adults how it was made and how it has been used.

When you come to the part of your service where you intercede for others, you can suggest three or four areas or subjects for prayer, and give a brief introduction to each. Then ask children (and adults) to imagine they are a homeless refugee, a frightened person awaiting an operation, and so on. What would they need God to be for them? Select a title from the wall, and pray for God to be that for them. Each situation could well need several of the titles from the wall.

This way of praying could encourage children to voice their

prayers in front of the whole church if they are able to use a simple formula such as 'Lord please come to the people in . . . as their . . . Amen.'

This Outline need not, of course, be restricted to Trinity Sunday.

72. God Is . . .

Aim

To encourage children to reflect on the many facets that make up the character of God.

Setting

Older children's groups and all-age services.

Equipment

A selection of about ten objects such as a rock, a shell, a floppy disk, a beautiful flower, a map, a glass bowl filled with water, etc.; a large piece of material; a CD player and some quiet instrumental music.

Outline

Arrange the objects on some material draped over a low table, or on the floor in the centre of the room, so that the display can be clearly seen by everyone. Introduce the activity by saying that there are very many biblical images of God and that those different pictures reveal different aspects of his nature. It is normal that individually we feel more comfortable with some images than others, but it is vital that we seek to develop as complete a picture of our God as we can in order to stay faithful to the God who is revealed in the Bible, rather than simply making him in our own image.

Explain that you are going to move into a prolonged period of quiet which will begin with a simple prayer inviting God to come and speak to individuals and reveal something about his character through one of the objects on display. During the quiet time it can be helpful to have some music playing softly to hide shuffles and other extraneous noises.

After five minutes or so invite any who are willing to share with the group the thoughts that they have had. It could be useful at this point to have Bibles on hand for people to refer to particular passages which may have come to mind. Use the contributions from the group to lead into a time of corporate sung worship. Songs which include several names for God could be useful, for example 'You are the mighty King', 'Jehovah jireh', and 'Jesus, name above all names'.

New School Year

No. 74 'A Hands-on Approach'

Although not strictly part of the liturgical calendar, the first Sunday in September can be a major landmark for young children starting school (this may happen at other times too, depending on your local authority), those moving to a new school, and of course teachers and other staff preparing for re-entry. We can use this Sunday as an opportunity to pray especially for our schools and for all those in education.

73. School Photos

Aim

To intercede creatively for local schools, and those who study and work in them.

Setting

All-age services.

Equipment

Photos of local schools, either taken yourself or from prospectuses.

Outline

This idea is very simple: to pray for local schools using pictures of them. The schools selected should include all of those to which your children go, and may include others if they are within your parish or 'catchment area'. You can include everything from nurseries to local universities: it's up to you.

The pictures can be shown in a variety of ways: you can use them to make static displays (this could be done in advance), or you could have them turned into acetates for OHP, or scan them into PowerPoint presentations, depending on the level of technological advancement in your church.

You could then use the pictures in different ways: you could move around static displays put in different places round the church. At each place those who go to or work in that school could share ten things for which to give thanks, and three points for prayer: these could be written down and added to the display for ongoing use. Alternatively, to save time, people could choose which display to go to, and you could pray in those groups at the same time.

If you are projecting the pictures centrally, go through them and get those involved in each school to come forward as their school is prayed for. You may like to lay hands on and pray especially for those starting a new school, or starting school for the first time.

So often our praying for school children is along the lines of 'protect them in this hostile environment'. Try to be a bit more positive, and pray that by their influence the school will be changed for the better. Pray for God's blessing, even on those people in the school you might find less than amenable to the gospel.

74. A Hands-on Approach

Aim

To pray for teachers and others who work in schools as they approach the new term.

Setting

All-age services.

Outline

Invite any teachers or others in your congregation who work in schools to come forward, and ask the children to lay hands on them, pray for them, and even prophesy over them. This can be a welcome addition to the more usual practice of adults praying for children.

75. Jesus Goes to School

Aim

To encourage the children to see Jesus in their school situations and to hear his words to them.

Setting

Children's groups.

Equipment

Copper or brass pot; tin of metal polish and wadding; clean cloth; CD-player and CD of quiet ambient music.

Outline

Before the session, rub the pot all over with the polish, but don't buff it up to a shine. Introduce the session with the help of a stooge who is wearing a clean (but not valuable!) white shirt. Get them to hold the pot for a while, so that when they finally put it down their hands and shirt are covered in black. Talk about school as a place where we are influenced: it is very easy to get 'dirty' from the things we hear, the people we spend time with, and so on.

Then give your helper a cloth and get them to polish up the pot so that it is clean and shiny. Talk about the fact that we also have the opportunity to influence others for good, but that it is generally much harder work.

As we prepare to go back to school, we want to influence others for good, and not become influenced ourselves in a negative way. Explain to the children that they're going to pray in a particular way, which will be easier if they close their eyes and let God show them pictures in their minds. Play some quiet music to cover coughs, shuffles and so on.

A leader should begin by inviting the Holy Spirit to come and help in this prayer time, and then the children may be led in a visualisation which starts from the door of their classroom. Tell them that Jesus is present beside them as they stand at the door looking in: some might 'see' his face or body, others might just be aware of a bright light, others may see nothing but nevertheless be aware of his presence.

Then invite the children to walk with Jesus into the room. In my experience various things might happen at this point, and the leader will need to be very open to the Spirit to discern what God might want to say or do. On one occasion there was a sense that God was walking around the school 'spring cleaning' it of all negative influences ready for the new intake of children, but it might be that God will show children particular faces of friends whom they might influence for the good, or others with whom they should tread warily.

Your imaginary walk might continue into the assembly hall, the playground, and other key areas of the campus. The idea is to encourage a dialogue between God and the children, with him speaking and showing them things but also with them asking him to be present in different aspects of their school life. You will need to gauge carefully the time all this takes: watch for signs that you're losing their attention and draw it to a close quickly.

You may want to arrange for a brief feedback session the following week for children to share stories about their awareness of God's presence during the week before.

Harvest

No. 84 'The "Wow!" Factor'

Harvest festivals have a long history, going back to Old Testament times, as opportunities to give thanks to God for his provision to us, particularly of crops and food. In rural communities 'harvest home' would have been a great celebration anyway, and combining thanks to God and a good knees-up would have seemed natural. Nowadays, when most children probably think milk comes from the supermarket rather than a cow, harvest has undergone some creative reinterpretations, but fundamentally it is about celebrating the partnership of human work and God's care and provision.

God has used the Green movement to open the eyes of Christians to what has been in the Bible all along – that his redemptive purposes are not just for men and women but for the whole of the created realm – and there is much more concern for the environment reflected in current liturgical and musical writing. Therefore themes such as creation, ecology and employment are most appropriately linked in with harvest, and the festival is commonly used to focus prayer and financial giving on those in lands of hunger and famine.

God must be kept at the centre, of course, to avoid the mistake Paul talks about in Romans 1 as the fundamental error of the human race: to worship created things rather than their Creator.

76. Sight and Sound

Aim

To add a new visual dimension to worship.

Setting

Children's groups or all-age services.

Equipment

Images of creation from books or a photo CD.

Outline

Make one or two acetates or PowerPoint backgrounds from your images, either by using a computer printer and inkjet acetates, or by taking paper copies of photos to your local copyprint bureau. The images should be of good enough quality to fill most of an A4 acetate.

When you project your worship songs using OHP, put your creation image acetate on first, and then lay the song words on top of it, so that the words are projected over an image which brings the words to life. If you use PowerPoint, or a similar presentation program, use your image as a slide background. For example, 'My Jesus, my Saviour' could be projected over a picture of mountains and seas.

Other more general effects can be achieved by overlaying your song acetate with bubblewrap, plain coloured film or other textured but transparent material. But if you just use hymnbooks ... sorry, we can't help!

77. Dolphin Music

Aim

To add impact to words or quiet times.

Setting

Children's groups or all-age services.

Equipment

CD or tape of natural sounds.

Outline

Rather than using music as a backdrop to silent meditation, you could use recordings of natural sounds such as waves breaking, birdsong and so on. You could also use such recordings to accompany the reading of a Psalm or other Bible passage, and some OHP visuals could make the experience even more multi-sensory, as well as providing a non-verbal focus for very young children.

It goes without saying that the focus of such meditations should be the Creator and not his creation.

The use of image and sound in this and the previous example can of course be extended to other aspects of worship: images of deserts or parched land could be shown while praying for those who are starving, and so on.

78. Harvest Hip-Hop

Aim

To write a modern-day Psalm or rap to express our gratitude to God for his bountiful provision.

Setting

Children's groups, or possibly a school setting.

Equipment

Items for displays as below; pencils; paper; possibly a drum machine or keyboard with drum rhythms.

Outline

Set up five different displays of things that God has provided for each of the senses: taste, touch, sight, hearing, smell.

Invite the children to choose one display and explore the items there by tasting, smelling, touching and so on. Use the display as a springboard to get them to talk about their favourite taste or sight or smell, etc. Then ask them to write a line or two of thanks for those things before moving on to a different display.

Eventually they should end up with a minimum of five ideas they could use as the basis for a 'thank you' Psalm or even a rap. They could work individually or in small groups, or they could even try to make a contribution reflecting the ideas of the whole group. Those with the right kind of expertise on hand could add drum beats and/or music.

If this is to be used as part of a bigger celebration it is probably most effective if done a week or two in advance to allow time for refinements and practice.

79. What a Load of Rubbish!

Aim

To discover God's concern about the things that pollute our lives.

Setting

All-age services or children's groups, but could also be used as a school assembly.

Equipment

Sweet papers; old drinks cans; newspaper; supermarket carrier bags, and so on.

Reading

Matthew 15:1–10.

Outline

Scatter your rubbish liberally around the floor, and talk about the environment, our lack of care for it, how this upsets God, etc. Make the point that pollution is a key issue about which more and more people are concerned.

Move on to talk about something which upsets God even more: the rubbish in our lives we can't see but which is there under the surface. Ask people to suggest some kinds of 'internal pollution' such as cheating, lying and so on.

Use some of these ideas to form prayers of confession, and as the physical rubbish is swept up and taken away, ask God to clean us up from the inside.

80. A Smashing Time

Aim

To help us feel something of what God feels about our ill-treatment of his creation.

Setting

All-age services or children's groups.

Equipment

Lego bricks.

Outline

Use all your creativity (or that of your children!) to construct a Lego model of your church or some other distinctive local building. Talk about how long it took to build, how proud you are of it, and so on.

Then get a child, previously primed, to drop and smash it deliberately while passing it around the group. Talk about how devastated you feel by his or her lack of care for what you have made.

Use this little scene to lead to confessing our lack of care for God's creation.

81. Do It Yourself

Aim

To give integrity to our worship by following it up with action.

Setting

All-age services.

Outline

Many churches collect food for a harvest display: it is then left to a few dedicated volunteers to take it round to old people's homes or needy areas for their annual handout.

Invite people to bring forward food to decorate the church in the usual way, but at the end of the service they should collect back again what they have brought, and take it to someone with whom they already have a relationship, with the good wishes of the church. Having prayed for needy people during the service, children (and adults) can be a part of the answer to their own prayers: having praised God for his provision they can join in with him in providing for others.

82. Out of the Mouths of Babes

Aim

To allow young children to join in with traditional hymns.

Setting

Younger children's groups, then the church service.

Outline

Harvest is one of those times when more established church-goers expect some traditional hymns, and sometimes feel cheated if they don't get them! But these hymns are rarely child-friendly, and can completely exclude very young children.

We took time in our groups for a few weeks before Harvest Thanksgiving to learn the chorus to 'We plough the fields and scatter'. When we used it on Harvest Sunday, children from three upwards could join in heartily with:

All good gifts around us are sent from heaven above.
Then thank the Lord, O thank the Lord for all his love.

You could use the same principle for Christmas ('O come let us adore him') and Easter (all those hymns with repeated 'Alleluias').

83.   Falling Leaves

Aim

To allow children to join in with creation's praise of God.

Setting

Younger children's groups.

Equipment

Paddling pool; large groundsheet; piles of dry autumn leaves.

Outline

Put the paddling pool in the centre of the groundsheet, and fill
it with the leaves. Encourage the children to run their hands
through them, feel them and enjoy them. Talk about the
colour, the different shapes and designs and so on.

Tell them that God made the things he created in this world
to praise him, and that although people can praise God, other
things can too. Throw a handful of leaves in the air, and watch
them dance down to the ground. Then let the children have a
go, and encourage them to imagine the leaves dancing in
praise of God.

By now there should be leaves everywhere, so play some
appropriate music to which the children can dance, treading
through the leaves on the groundsheet, perhaps throwing
some more in the air as they dance. This whole exercise fills

children with a renewed sense of awe and wonder, which they may articulate as 'Wow!' This can lead you on to the next idea . . .

84. The 'Wow!' Factor

Aim

To share with the rest of the church young children's excitement about God and his creation.

Setting

Younger children's groups, and then the whole church.

Equipment

Large sheet of card or frieze paper; PVA glue and spreaders; dry autumn leaves.

Outline

Following on from Outline No. 83, you could share the excitement with the rest of the church by making a leafy 'Wow!' picture. (Wow is a three-year-old's equivalent of 'Praise the Lord!') Stick the leaves onto the paper in the shape of a huge 'Wow!', add it to your harvest display, and maybe share with the church the story behind its creation.

85. Patchwork Praise

Aim

To create a display to aid praise to God for his provision for us.

Setting

Younger children's groups, and possibly an all-age service.

Equipment

Hexagonal pieces of paper or card in different bright colours; large piece of frieze paper; felt pens; PVA glue and spreaders.

Outline

Although this idea works well at Harvest time, it could be used on any occasion as an aid to praise and worship. Talk with the children about all the lovely things God has given to us to enjoy, and get them to identify some of their favourite things, preferably associated with colours. Some examples might be bright red apples, my new blue dress, brown autumn leaves, green cabbage (unlikely, that one!), and so on.

Get each child to choose a hexagon the same colour as their favourite thing, and either draw or write on it, with help from the adults. You might want each child to choose two or three colours, according to the size of the group.

You can then stick the hexagons onto the large piece of

paper in the style of a patchwork quilt, talking as you do so about each object, why they love it so much, how good God is to provide it, and so on. The finished quilt can be displayed and used as a visual aid during a time of sung or spoken worship.

Alternatively, having started work on the quilt during their group time, the children could then return to the main service with the quilt partially finished and encourage the rest of the congregation to add to it with their favourite coloured things, so that the quilt can be displayed before the whole church to aid their praise. Appropriate songs might include 'God is good, God is great', or 'Thank you very much'.

Gift Day

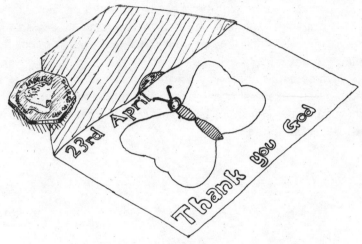

No. 86 'Envelopes'

Many churches have an annual Gift Day, either for their own funds or to give away to mission at home and/or overseas. There are also specific projects, such as building improvements, for which special gifts are asked. Yet rarely are children included in these events: they are either deliberately excused, as a matter of church policy, or else it never even occurs to anyone to include them.

My policy has always been to encourage children to give proportionately and at times sacrificially, on the basis that while their pocket money tithe won't revolutionise church finances now, if they can get into giving as a habit, when they grow up to be managing directors, the church could benefit greatly! And of course giving is part of Christian discipleship:

just because some adults shirk that responsibility, there is no reason to teach children not to give.

I also encourage children to begin early on to think responsibly about their own money, rather than asking parents for money for the collection just before they leave home. And of course we have encouraged the children to be completely open with parents about the church policy over giving, so that they can co-operate with their children's learning. For example, we always gave our children their pocket money in the right coins such that they could easily extract ten per cent for their gift envelopes.

So ignore the cries of your treasurer that it is too much bother to open a load of envelopes with a few pence in, or that the cost of the envelopes is greater than the amount in them: invest for the future!

86. Envelopes

Aim

To encourage the children to give regularly through the church envelope scheme.

Setting

Children's groups.

Equipment

Paper; small envelopes; felt pens.

Reading

1 Corinthians 16; 2 Corinthians 8–9.

Outline

Teach about the importance of regular giving. Children can then design their own offering envelope designs, which can be scanned later and printed onto inkjet labels and stuck onto plain envelopes.

Their designs can include their names, or, if anonymity is a concern, they can be allocated numbers by your treasurer as the adults are. Use the envelopes each week to engender a sense of pride and joy in giving. The church leaders will ideally make sure that the offering is seen as a part of the church's worship, and take it up while the children are present in church, not while they are out in their groups. Alternatively, if you take up an offering within the children's groups, this should be handled as an act of worship.

87. Envelopes, but not Stationary!

Aim

To make giving fun.

Setting

Children's groups, or an all-age service if you think you can get away with it!

Equipment

Large collection plate or bowl; money.

Outline

Take up the offering African-style: instead of passing plates round the church while the people stay where they are, put a large plate at the front and get everyone to process past it and put in their envelope or money. Use a lively song, possibly with an African flavour, and encourage children to dance, not walk, around the church. Keep the music going until all have passed by the plate, then offer it to God for use in his kingdom.

88. Kids' Packs

Aim

To encourage children to be fully a part of the church's Gift Day.

Setting

Children's groups.

Equipment

Gift Day packs, suitably adapted.

Outline

Many churches produce some kind of information pack for their projects or Gift Days. Work with the church finance department to produce child-friendly versions of the adults' packs, which give the same basic information, but in a way that children, with the help of their leaders and parents, can read and understand. Use simpler words, larger print, lots of clip-art, and make the range of responses appropriate (they probably won't pay by direct debit!).

Use one morning for a big 'launch' in your groups, talk through the project(s) so that the children know what they're giving to, and so that they can feel some sense of involvement and ownership. Pray and listen to God about their responses, and tell them to go home and talk to their parents about what they feel God is saying. Spend some time in worship to the God who gives so much for us.

All Saints

No. 90 'On Yer Bike'

All Saints is celebrated on November 1st, and it is the time when we remember those who have gone before us in the Christian faith, thanking God for their example and inspiration to us who are still here on earth. The liturgical colour is white or gold.

The issue of the saints is a controversial one: many fear, quite rightly, lest we should slip into praying *to* them, and of course the New Testament is quite clear that all Christians are saints: there is no premier league of superheroes. Nevertheless, Christians have found it helpful down the ages, in running their own race, to seek encouragement from the example of the great cloud of witnesses who have run with perseverance the race marked out for them, while all the time fixing their eyes on Jesus (Hebrews 12).

All Saints allows us to concentrate on the present as well as the future: all of us who are disciples of Jesus have our part to play now, in the company of all who believe in him and are working for his kingdom. We gain encouragement not just from heroes of the past, but also from those around us today.

We have not in this book suggested material for individual Saints' Days, but there is a wealth of background material available, for example in books like *The Penguin Dictionary of Saints*, and the *Oxford Dictionary of the Christian Church*.

89. Passing the Baton

Aim

To encourage the children to give thanks for all those down the years who have passed the Christian inheritance on to us, and to see ourselves as the latest in the line of saints who have the task of passing the Good News on to the next generation.

Setting

Children's groups.

Equipment

Batons; cards; felt pens.

Reading

Hebrews 12:1–3.

Outline

Begin by dividing the children into teams for a relay race in which they have a baton which has to be passed to the next person in the team before they can set off.

Talk about the disciples, who were the first people Jesus entrusted with the baton of the Good News, and then the early Christians who told the next generation, and so on down the years. You could make special mention of any local saints.

End by bringing things right up to date and ask the children to think about people who have been significant in their own Christian growth.

Encourage the children to pray 'thank you' prayers for those who have helped them to faith. Then go on to make 'thank you' cards which they can give or send to those same people to say 'thank you for showing me Jesus'.

You could tell the children stories of other children whom God has used in bringing people to him, or it could be that there are some stories that members of the group could share from their personal experience. Then move on to a time when the children pray for one another, asking God to come and empower them with all they need to pass the baton on to the next generation. Ask for sensitivity to see the opportunities in front of them and boldness to take them.

The worship songs could contain thanks for friends and church family, and you could also use prayerful songs like 'Jesus touch me now', 'Come Lord Jesus' (chorus from 'Great is the darkness') or 'Be bold, be strong'.

90. On Yer Bike!

Aim

To help us recognise that we all have a contribution to make in the body of Christ, and to give thanks for our gifts and those of others.

Setting

All-age services or children's groups.

Equipment

A small tool or other useful item for everyone in the group/congregation. You should include a bicycle with a flat tyre and everything necessary for mending a puncture.

Reading

1 Corinthians 12:12–31.

Outline

Have some fun talking about the items that everyone has been given. Then have someone come in with a bicycle with a flat tyre that needs mending before they can go home. Explain that you'd love to help but you only have a pencil sharpener in your pocket and that's not a lot of use when it comes to mending tyres.

Turn to the group and say, 'What we really need is a tyre lever to get the tyre off the wheel. I don't suppose anyone has one?' Go through the whole process of mending the puncture, with each item required being supplied by unsuspecting members of the congregation.

Draw the comparison with the body of Christ: none of us has all the gifts but between us we have everything we need. However, we need everyone to make their distinctive contribution in order to get the job done. Take the opportunity to build one another up by thanking individuals for being a part of the body where you are. Lead into some sung worship thanking God for one another and then move on to pray for each other.

91. For All the Saints

Aim

To teach that all Christians are saints, and to encourage one another and build up relationships across the age groups.

Setting

Children's groups.

Equipment

Flipchart and pens; felt pens and card.

Outline

Do some teaching on the way the New Testament uses the term 'saint', not for a superhero but for all Christians. Then brainstorm a list of all the saints in your church, and what they each do in service to the church. Collect these on the flipchart, and help the children out with the less obvious ones: they can see clearly who's in the worship team, but they may have no idea who the treasurer is, or even what a treasurer is!

Invite the Holy Spirit to come and highlight for each child one person/job from the list on the flipchart, and then get them to make a card for that person, addressed to 'Saint Fred' or whoever, thanking them for all they do for the church in their particular role. The children can give them out personally over coffee after the service.

While the children are doing this, the adults can be encouraged, in their service, to think of someone who has been a significant influence to them in their Christian life, but with whom they have now lost touch. They can be encouraged to write and say 'thank you' to those people.

92. Local Heroes

Aim

To discover something about the life of God's followers from the past, to thank God for them, and to be inspired by their ministry.

Setting

Children's groups, and all-age services.

Outline

Many churches (not just Anglican ones) are dedicated to or named after a saint, or maybe your town or area has a local saint about whom you can discover some information. Each saint has a date attached to them, often the date of their death, and Anglican churches often celebrate a 'patronal festival' on that date or a Sunday near it.

Spend time in your children's groups discovering something about your saint's life, and plan an all-age service to celebrate him or her as creatively as you can with songs, displays, readings and so on. The nature of your saint will dictate what you might appropriately do. But make sure you emphasise that we are all saints, according to the New Testament, and that the heroes from the past are there not to be worshipped, but rather as good examples, for whom we can praise God and from whom we can learn and gain inspiration.

Christ the King

No. 94 'Reign in Me'

This festival, which is celebrated on the Sunday before Advent begins, is a real young upstart in the church calendar, having been founded by the church in 1925 as a protest against the growing trend towards dictatorships in Europe. As late as 1970 it was put onto its current date before Advent. Since the new church year begins on Advent Sunday, it seems fitting to close the old year with a look towards the future, and to celebrate the final, eternal and all-encompassing triumph of Christ, and his reign for ever and ever.

There is obviously some overlap with the themes of Ascension, and many of the suggestions in this book are inter-changeable between the two occasions, but there is a subtle difference: Ascension celebrates Christ's reign before he returns to earth, and therefore his work of intercession for us

229

as we struggle on (see Hebrews 4, 5 and 10), whereas Christ the King is focused more on the final and eternal reign of Jesus. As such it is an opportunity to look forward to our ultimate destiny as we reign with him. The liturgical colour is either red or white/gold.

93. King of Kings

Aim

To add a visual dimension to our celebration of Jesus, the King of kings.

Setting

All-age services or children's groups.

Equipment

Sheets of A3 paper with 'Jesus: King of Kings' written on them in outline or bubble writing; lots of shiny paper, such as toffee wrappers; metallic gummed shapes, etc.; PVA glue and spreaders.

Outline

As people arrive, get them into groups and invite them to make a collage on their sheet, so that the words stand out. They'll need to work very quickly, and make sure that even the youngest of children can contribute. Worship music could be played in the background.

Leave the sheets to dry while the service proceeds, but as a climax to your worship, while singing something like 'Welcome King of kings', 'He is the King of kings', or 'Hosanna', use the pictures like banners to lift up every time you sing the words 'Jesus' or 'King of kings'.

94. Reign in Me

Aim

To allow children to respond to the need to let Jesus reign supremely in their lives.

Setting

Children's groups.

Equipment

Coloured card; scissors; sellotape or stapler; felt pens; gummed coloured shapes; an armchair or similar, covered and made to look like a throne possibly on a dais.

Outline

Make some crowns, as in Outline No. 96, but instead of characteristics of Jesus encourage them to write on their crowns things which might be especially important to them. You might get ideas like 'my bike', 'a new Dreamcast', 'Manchester United', 'Barbie', and so on.

Explain to the children that in the past it was a mark of respect and submission to take off your crown and lay it at the feet of a conquering king: you can read about a similar act in Revelation 4:10. Challenge the children to take off their crowns and lay them at the foot of the throne to symbolise that Jesus is more important to them than all these other things.

They could then pray for one another in groups, with simple laying on of hands and prayers like 'Lord, please come and be King in Jenny's life. Amen,' or 'Lord, please take the place of Jimmy's . . . as the most important thing in his life. Amen.'

95. Kings and Queens

Aim

To encourage different appropriate expressions of worship to Jesus the King.

Setting

Children's groups or all-age services.

Outline

Tell the children to imagine that the Queen is coming to visit your local High Street or shopping precinct. How would they act if they were in the crowd? Collect ideas such as waving flags, shouting, cheering, clapping, etc.

Then tell them to imagine she is coming to their church and wants to meet each of them personally, one at a time. How would they come into her presence this time? (Humbly, quietly, reverently, etc.)

Both are appropriate given the different settings, and the same is true of meeting King Jesus: sometimes we shout and sing as part of a crowd, but sometimes we are quiet and reverent.

Use some songs which move from one kind of worship to the other. A song slot might include: 'Welcome, King of kings', 'Blessed is the King who comes', 'I will worship' and 'Lord and Father, King forever'. 'Lord we've come to worship you' and 'I raise my hands up high' are songs which express both aspects of worship.

96. King? What King?

Aim

To celebrate different character aspects of Jesus the King.

Setting

Children's groups.

Equipment

Coloured card; scissors; sellotape or stapler; felt pens; gummed coloured shapes.

Outline

Give the children a brief age-appropriate account of some good kings and bad kings, from English history or the Old Testament. Brainstorm what sort of king Jesus would be, from their knowledge of him through the Bible and their own personal experience.

Help each child to make a crown, and to write on it (easier before it's formed into a circle!) 'Jesus is a . . . king', choosing a word from your brainstorm which has personal significance for them. Then decorate the crowns with gummed shapes.

During a time of praise, invite the children to form simple prayers along the lines of 'Thank you, Jesus, that you are a ... king'. The reinforcement through craft work of these theological truths means that they should stay with the children, and could lead on to some group storytelling about times when Jesus has been kind, powerful, and so on, to them.

97. Stained-Glass Windows

Aim

To worship Jesus as King and to produce a card or picture befitting the glory of the King.

Setting

Older children's groups (this will take two sessions, to allow drying time between).

Equipment

Clip frames or OHP acetates for each child; glass paint and outliner (available from craft shops); thin paintbrushes; cardboard frames; CD player and ambient music.

Outline

Begin by talking about kingship: what a king looks like; the type of clothes a king would wear; colours connected with royalty; items associated with reigning – thrones, sceptres, orbs; the richness of their possessions, for example gold cups and plates, and so on.

Having introduced the theme in this way, go on to say that today we are going to celebrate Jesus, our King. If people on earth can create this kind of splendour and glory for earthly kings to enjoy, how much better must Jesus' throne in heaven be? Invite the children to close their eyes and use their imaginations as they listen to you reading passages from Revelation 4 and 5. Read slowly and allow space for them to visualise the things you read. It could be helpful to have some ambient music playing quietly as you read, and to allow some space at the end for individuals to make their own response to God either in silence or in spoken prayers of praise. Continue this time of worship by singing songs like 'Majesty', 'He is exalted', 'You are the mighty King' or 'Lord and Father, King forever'. You could include a time of singing in tongues as well.

Explain to the children that they are going to move on and continue their worship by creating pictures to express their appreciation of the glory of King Jesus. Each child will need a piece of paper the same size as the piece of glass or acetate on which they will do their painting, and they should begin by drawing their design onto the paper in pencil. They could draw a crown or a letter 'J', or any other design that they feel inspired to draw.

When they are happy with their design, they should put their sheet of glass or acetate over it, and trace the outline by squeezing the black outliner paint onto the glass. This will resemble the lead of a stained-glass window. This is the end of stage one, and the windows must be left until dry (it takes about twenty-four hours), so you will probably need to continue at your next session.

The windows are completed next time by filling in the spaces between the outlines with different coloured glass paint, using thin brushes. If you've used thin acetate, the windows will need to be mounted in a card frame. The finished products can be taken home as reminders of the worship experience the children have enjoyed, and as an aid to future worship.

Missions

No. 99 '. . . and Going'

Although there is no set date for it in the church calendar, many churches keep special Sundays when their focus is on mission, particularly overseas. This may be a regular annual event, or it may happen from time to time when a mission partner is on furlough, or when new missionaries are being sent out. These two ideas can help children to engage creatively with those working for God in other cultures, and can encourage ongoing prayer and support.

98. Coming . . .

Aim

To help the children to know how to begin to pray for someone leaving to become a missionary.

Setting

Children's groups, whole congregation, school assembly.

Equipment

Items as below; a tray or table to display them; a cloth or
sheet; pencils and paper.

Outline

Gather together a selection of about twenty items which are in
some way connected with the missionary situation. They
could be items the person will need, such as water purifying
tablets or a mosquito net, tools they'll need to do their job
when they get there, or items relating to the place where they
are going, such as local crafts or produce.

Briefly talk through each item in turn, and include some
related prayer need. Then cover the items with a cloth and ask
the children, either individually or in small groups, to write
down as many of the items as they can remember. After a few
minutes reveal the items again and see who has listed the
most. (Many of the children will know this as 'Kim's Game'.)

Then spend some time in small groups praying for the missionary.

You may wish to end the session by having a number of the children lay hands on a visiting missionary and pray for them as people rather than their ministries or callings, listening to God for words and/or pictures to encourage them.

Songs speaking of God's presence with us (such as 'Be bold, be strong' and 'God is the one') or the call to serve ('The Servant King' and 'I want to serve the purpose of God') could be appropriate to use.

99. . . . and Going

Aim

To involve the congregation, but especially children, in the sending out of someone for the first time to another country.

Setting

An all-age service or children's group.

Equipment

Ethnic food and music; pictures and other items relating to your chosen country.

Outline

Try to create a worship time based on the country to which your missionary has been called, or is already working.

People will need advance warning of this but invite every-one to come dressed (albeit stereotypically!) in something appropriate to that country. Have some ethnic food and music available. Try to learn a few significant words of the lan-guage, and maybe even have a go at singing a worship song in that language. Give thanks to God for the good things that come from that country, for example some of the things you've just eaten, or the national characteristics which enrich the whole world.

Pray for the people of the other land. Sing an extra verse of

'I'm special', changing the words to 'They're special', and ask the congregation to hold a picture of the people in their minds. If your architecture and technology permit, you could even turn a photograph of some people from that country into an OHP acetate to underlay the words of the song, or use it as a PowerPoint background.

Pray and lay hands on the missionary. Listen to any words of encouragement or pictures God may give for them. Ask God what kind of on-going support he may be asking you to make, individually or as a children's group, church or school.

100. So I Send You

Aim

To help to make the Great Commission something that the children can begin to see working out in their own lives.

Setting

Children's groups.

Equipment

Cards; felt pens.

Reading

Matthew 28:16–20.

Outline

Talk about how last words are often important. One example would be the last words Mum says before she leaves you: 'Be good'. The last words Jesus said to his followers were something like 'Go and make more like you. And I'll go with you and help you do it.'

Ask the children to be quiet and ask God to show them one friend, neighbour or family member who doesn't know Jesus as their friend and who God would like them to help get to know him. He might just tell them a name, they might see a face in their mind's eye, or they might remember something that person has done with them or said in the past.

Having identified someone, each child can make and decorate a card with a short prayer for that person. They can take it home and keep it in a place where they will see it regularly and so be reminded to pray for them. If time is short the cards could be prepared in advance with space for the children simply to fill in their person's name. The prayer could be something like 'Dear Jesus, thank you that you love . . . . Please help . . . to get to know you as a friend. Please help me to show . . . your love. Amen.'

This section could conclude with a time of sung worship, using for example 'Jesus touch me now' and 'We want to see Jesus lifted high'. Opportunity could be given for the children to pray for one another, asking God to come and fill them with his Spirit and empower them to show God's love to their friend.

Subject Index

Numbers refer to Outlines not pages.

Baptism   20, 68
Birthdays   8, 62

Character of God   19, 45,
    58, 59, 70, 71, 72, 94
Church   15, 62, 66, 89, 90,
    91
Commitment   16, 20, 21,
    23, 31, 43, 47, 94
Confession   27, 29, 30, 32,
    34, 43, 47, 79, 80
Creation   32, 59, 76, 77, 79,
    80, 83, 84

Discipleship   16, 21

Encouragement   15, 24, 53,
    58, 68, 89, 90, 91
Evangelism   18, 40, 73, 89,
    100

Fear   14, 40

Fire   67
Freedom   30

Giving   7, 16, 23, 81, 86,
    87, 88

Heaven   3, 59, 89, 97
Holy Spirit   63, 66, 67, 68
Hope   12, 13, 14

Jesus, God's Son   22
Jesus the King   55, 56, 60,
    93, 94, 95, 96, 97

Missionary activities   17,
    98, 99

Names of God   70, 71

Persecution   40
Perseverance   58, 89, 91
Pilgrimage   2, 13, 14, 25

Prayer for the world   17, 32,
  46, 71, 77, 99

Repentance   26, 27, 30, 31,
  34

Saints   89, 92
Saying 'thank you'   9, 10,
  25, 35, 36, 37, 62, 78, 84,
  85, 91
School   73, 74

Senses   78
Serving others   18, 36, 37,
  42, 81, 91
Sin   29, 31, 32, 34, 43, 80
Spiritual gifts   64, 65, 90

Tongues   65
Trinity   69, 72

Waiting   3, 4, 59
Wind   63, 66

Song Index

A list of songs quoted, with sources.

Amazing Love ....SF 398

Be bold, be strong..SFK 6
Blessed is the King who comes....................................ISH USA 2

Christmas, it's Christmas ....KS 26
Come on and celebrate ....SFK 17

Don't let my love grow cold ....TS 81

Faithful one so unchanging ....SF 89
Father we love you ....SF 102
For the joys and for the sorrows ....TS 110

God is good, God is great ....KS 73
God is the one who wants the best for me ....KS 79
God's not dead ....SFK 49
Great is the darkness ....TS 136
Great is the Lord and most worthy of praise ....SF 145

He has risen! ....TS 155
He is exalted ....SF 164

He is the King of kings ....SF 57
He walked where I walk ....TS 168
Hear O Lord our cry ....SF 158
Heaven invites you to a party ....TS 150
Hosanna ....KS 111

I am a new creation ....KS 115
I just want to live to please you (Take my life, Lord) .....SLC 12
I raise my hands up high ....SLC 14
I want to serve the purpose of God ....SF 260
I will offer up my life ....KS 186
I will worship ....TS 270
I'm special ....SFK 92

Jehovah jireh ....KS 190
Jesus Christ (Once again) ....KS 192
Jesus is the name we honour ....TS 285
Jesus isn't dead anymore ....KS 198
Jesus' love is very wonderful ....KS 208
Jesus, name above all names ....SF 298
Jesus send me the helper ....KS 213
Jesus touch me now ....KS 215
Jesus we celebrate your victory ....SFK 117
Jesus we enthrone you ....SF 310

Lord and Father, King forever ....SF 350
Lord be in my mind ....SLC 38
Lord, have mercy on us ....TS 328
Lord I lift your name on high ....KS 234
Lord Jesus I love you ....SLC 27
Lord take away my sin ....SLC 28
Lord we've come to worship you ....KS 241

Majesty ....KS 246
Make me a channel of your peace ....SFK 135
My Jesus my Saviour ....KS 257

O Lord your tenderness ....SF 433
Over all the earth (Reign in me again) ....SH 102

Praise and glory to the name of Jesus ....SLC 30

Shine, Jesus, shine ....SFK 127
Spirit of the living God ....SFK 161

Thank you for saving me ....TS 472
Thank you Jesus ....SFK 162
Thank you very much ....KS 314
The Servant King ....KS 62
This little light of mine ....KS 343

We are marching (Siya Hamba) ....KS 350
We bow down ....SH 135
We want to see Jesus lifted high ....KS 365
We worship you, Father, Son and Holy Spirit ....KS 367
Welcome, King of kings ....TS 548
What a wonderful Saviour is Jesus ....SFK 39
Whether you're one or whether you're two ....KS 384
Why do you look here for the living? ....ISH USA 14

You are the mighty King ....SF 628
You laid aside your majesty ....SF 633

Key

ISH USA *Ishmael USA* songbook (Thankyou Music Ltd, P.O. Box 75, Eastbourne, E. Sussex BN23 6NW).

KS   *Kidsource* compiled by Capt Alan Price (Kevin Mayhew Ltd, Buxhall, Stowmarket, Suffolk IP14 3DJ).

SF   *Songs of Fellowship* (Kingsway Music, Lottbridge Drove, Eastbourne, E. Sussex BN23 6NT).

SFK *Songs of Fellowship for Kids* (Kingsway Music, Lottbridge Drove, Eastbourne, E. Sussex BN23 6NT).

SH *Spring Harvest Praise 2000* (Spring Harvest, 14 Horsted Square, Uckfield, E. Sussex TN22 1QL).

SLC *Ishmael's Songs for Little Children* (available from Revelation Centre, P.O. Box 58, Chichester, W. Sussex PO19 2UD).

TS *The Source,* compiled by Graham Kendrick (Kevin Mayhew Ltd, Rattlesden, Bury-St-Edmunds, Suffolk IP30 0SZ).

Other useful liturgical resources

Patterns for Worship (Church House Publishing, Church House, Great Smith Street, London SW1P 3NZ).

The Promise of His Glory (jointly published by Church House Publishing and Mowbray, a Cassell imprint).

Lent, Holy Week, Easter: Services and Prayers (jointly published by Church House Publishing, Cambridge University Press, The Pitt Building, Trumpington Street, Cambridge CB2 1RP and SPCK, Holy Trinity Church, Marylebone Road, London NW1 4DU).

100 Instant Ideas for All-Age Worship

by Sue Relf

Having people of all ages together for any length of structured time can be a challenge. This book provides a wealth of 'pick and mix' ideas for those involved in leading all-age worship, including:

- mini-talks
- dramas
- Bible readings
- raps
- praise and worship
- prayers
- testimonies
- quizzes

100 Creative Prayer Ideas for Children

by Jan Dyer

Children are made in the image of a Creator God,
and they enjoy being creative themselves! So it makes
sense to use a variety of ways to stimulate children to
develop their prayer lives. That way they can build a
meaningful friendship with him that will last a lifetime.

Jan Dyer has provided an array of tried and tested
ideas, divided into ten areas of a child's life:

- family life
- school life
- friends
- my neighbourhood
- my country
- the world
- myself
- creation
- God's work
- God's word

CHILDREN'S
MINISTRY

100 Simple Bible Craft Ideas for Children

by Sue Price

Many of us learn more effectively when we have something to see and something to make; when we can interact rather than simply sit and listen. Crafts can therefore be used as a vital part of any session with children, and not just an add-on.

This collection of illustrated ideas has been specifically designed to help children learn stories and truths from the Bible in such a way that they can make them part of their lives. They are ideal for teachers who would not regard themselves as experts, yet can easily be adapted by the more experienced!

The ideas have been grouped according to categories:

- Bible stories
- lesson reminders
- aids to worship
- crafts to give
- seasonal items

The result is a ready-to-use collection that will prove invaluable to anyone who plays a part in the teaching of children.

50 Musical Activities for Children

by Alison Hedger

These delightful songs with accompanying teaching ideas are a simple but fun way to teach biblical wisdom to the children in your group.

The subject index covers themes from disappointment to faith, from anger to love. Simple instructions are given on helping children to understand the basics of tempo, and there are even some home-made instruments that can be made without breaking the bank.

Includes full score to all songs and free CD.

ALISON HEDGER is a primary school music specialist and a composer of educational musicals. She describes herself as a trained musician who has spent her life doing what she likes most – making music with children.